EVALUATION RESOURCE HANDBOOK: GATHERING, ANALYZING, REPORTING DATA

by

B. FLAVIAN UDINSKY, Ed.D
STEVEN J. OSTERLIND, Ph.D.
SAMUEL W. LYNCH, Ph.D.

Department of Curriculum and Instruction
School of Education
University of Southern California
Los Angeles, California

EdITS publishers
San Diego, California 92107

83 - 8581

First Printing, August, 1981

ISBN: 0-912736-2-24-0

Library of Congress catalog card number: 81-065479

INTRODUCTION

This resource syllabus is directed towards providing student or practitioner with the tools necessary to implement evaluation. The thirty-nine articles contained herein have been written around topics which are commonly used in gathering, analyzing, and reporting data. The articles are themselves arranged into eight categories for similarity of purpose, technique, or information. The articles are written in outline format for ease of reference.

Each article is a compendium of research on the issue being considered. Few of the thoughts expressed in the articles are original to the authors. However, the authors believe it is unique to gather the salient points on an issue into one outlined article format. Verbiage is eschewed; instead, only succinct statements are included, followed, in many cases, by examples derived from the real-world experience of the authors. It is important to note that each article is followed by a carefully selected bibliography of the most useful and complete references readily available. While many of the articles address themselves to statistical issues, no statistical formulas or numerical computations are included. The reader is referred in each instance to several statistical texts or reference sources for this information.

Finally, it is not the authors' intention to provide a comprehensive overview of issues and thoughts on evaluation. It is their hope, however, that the evaluation issues selected are presented in a format useful to persons concerned with implementing the evaluation—persons who are likely to have a need to learn about procedures for gathering, analyzing, and reporting data.

TABLE OF CONTENTS

                                             Page

INTRODUCTION iv

Unit

I.   COMPETENCIES, ETHICS, AND ISSUES 1

          ISSUES INVOLVED WITH EVALUATION 3

          STANDARDS AND ETHICS 11

          ESSENTIAL TASKS AND COMPETENCIES IN
              RESEARCH AND EVALUATION 15

          COMPETENCIES AND QUALIFICATIONS FOR
              RESEARCH IN SCHOOLS 23

II.   PROBLEM SOLVING TECHNIQUES 27

          BRAINSTORMING 29

          DELPHI TECHNIQUE 33

          FORCE FIELD ANALYSIS 41

          TASK ANALYSIS 45

          Q-SORT TECHNIQUE 49

          NEEDS ASSESSMENT 53

III.   DATA CLASSIFICATION 57

          LEVELS OF MEASUREMENT 59

          VARIABLES 63

          SAMPLING 69

          FACTOR ANALYSIS 75

IV.   QUALITY CONTROL 81

          RESEARCH DESIGNS 83

          SOURCES OF ERRORS 91

          RELIABILITY AND VALIDITY 97

          ITEM ANALYSIS 101

          TEST ITEM BIAS 105

          FORMULATING HYPOTHESES 109

V.   DATA GATHERING TECHNIQUES 115
       THE QUESTIONNAIRE. 117
       THE INTERVIEW. 127
       PARTICIPANT OBSERVATION 137
       UNOBTRUSIVE MEASURES 143
       OBSERVATION TECHNIQUES 151
       MULTIPLE CRITERION MEASURES FOR
           EVALUATION OF SCHOOL PROGRAMS. 155

VI.   DEVELOPING SCALES. 159
       THURSTONE OR EQUAL INTERVAL SCALE 161
       LIKERT SCALE. 165
       GUTTMAN SCALE OR SCALOGRAM ANALYSIS. 169
       SEMANTIC DIFFERENTIAL 173
       NORM-REFERENCED MEASUREMENTS VERSUS
           CRITERION-REFERENCED MEASUREMENTS 177

VII.   DATA ANALYSIS 189
       STATISTICS 191
       CORRELATION. 197
       ANALYSIS OF VARIANCE 205
       ITEM RESPONSE THEORY: RASCH MODEL
           FOR TESTING CALIBRATIONS. 209
       CROSS TABULATION 213
       STATISTICAL PACKAGES 219

VIII.   REPORTING RESULTS. 223
       EXPRESSING TEST RESULTS. 225
       EVALUATION REPORTING FORMAT 231

BIBLIOGRAPHY 235

NAME INDEX 243

SUBJECT INDEX 246

UNIT I

COMPETENCIES, ETHICS, AND ISSUES

                                                                    Page

ISSUES INVOLVED WITH EVALUATION   3

STANDARDS AND ETHICS   11

ESSENTIAL TASKS AND COMPETENCIES IN
        RESEARCH AND EVALUATION 15

COMPETENCIES AND QUALIFICATIONS FOR
        RESEARCH IN SCHOOLS 23

ISSUES INVOLVED WITH EVALUATION

The evaluator should be aware that the utilization of evaluation findings becomes a key concern primarily when evaluation is viewed as part of a process of planned change. Educators who entertain a predisposition toward gradual and moderate change will evidence an interest in the outcomes of evaluation. For those for whom change is undesirable or impossible, and who view themselves as guardians of societal institutions, evaluation commands little interest.

Groups demanding rapid and radical change are also unlikely consumers of evaluation findings since their inclinations are likely to be ideological rather than empirical; evaluation does not respond to their information needs rapidly enough.

Evaluation involves judgments concerning administrative units, practitioners, programs, recipients of services, cost effectiveness, etc. Such judgments invariably produce real or imagined resentment from those who view themselves as being judged. The evaluator should be mindful of such human reactions, remembering that the issues addressed by evaluations and the manner in which results are reported are strongly related to sponsorship.

A. PROBLEMS OF ESTABLISHMENT

1. Decision makers have not accorded evaluative research a major role in policy formation and change in social programming (Rossi, 1969).

    a. Administrators, satisfied with informal evaluation, have often included evaluative research only when it was required by the funding agency.

    b. Some administrators may consider evaluative research expensive or of little practical value.

    c. Administrators may also have important covert reasons for resisting evaluative research:

(1) The presence of an evaluation component may invite administrators to consider the possibility that their policies do not lead
to effective realization of announced objectives.

(2) Because administrative claims for programs are usually extremely optimistic, evaluation results are almost inevitably
disappointing (Rossi, op. cit.).

2. Campbell (1969) observed that ambiguous results help to protect
administrators where there is a possibility of failure.

3. Freely available facts might reduce the privacy and security of some
administrators, making them vulnerable to inquiries about their honesty
and efficiency.

4. Administrators may resent evaluators who raise questions about basic
organizational premises or suggest evaluative criteria which may be
embarrassing to the organization.

5. Social scientists often demand preferential treatment which is resented
by other employees.

6. Social scientists, presuming superior wisdom on their part, may seek
direct access to top decision makers, thereby threatening bureaucrats
who are bypassed.

7. Social scientists, wishing to publicize their work, resent the norm of
secrecy prevailing in most organizations (Horowitz, 1969).

8. Social scientists may not wish to work within the framework of established policy and may want to challenge an agency's ideological
premises.

9. Some social scientists are concerned that agreement to undertake the
evaluation of a program may be interpreted as implicit commitment to
the philosophy or goals of that program; they may give it a legitimacy
they do not believe it deserves.

B. PROBLEMS OF ADMINISTRATION

1. Social scientists typically insist that ultimate responsibility for research
design and execution is theirs, even though they often advocate exten-
sive collaboration and communication with administrators.

2. Because evaluation is linked to top administration and generally involves examination of the activities of staff subordinates, evaluators
are sometimes viewed as tools of the administration—management spies.

3. Staff practitioners, interested in avoiding criticism of their work, are
likely to conceal real or imagined shortcomings, thereby invalidating
much data.

4. Scriven (1967) feels that the skepticism often exhibited by evaluative
researchers might dampen the creativity of a productive group.

5. The purely mechanical demands of data collection may also create a burden, particularly for the practitioner who, perhaps correctly, considers himself overburdened with record keeping.

6. When a research design calls for action inconsistent with immediate service goals, practitioners may disregard research/evaluation needs in favor of providing services.

7. Different conceptions of efficient use of time may lead to mutual annoyance.

   a. A professional evaluator is not accustomed to turning in daily time sheets, and his failure to do so may be interpreted as a sign of indolence by an administrator with time and cost concerns.

   b. Thinking is not a tangible use of time and could not be accepted in an agency which measured work in terms of clients interviewed, data gathered, meetings attended, and pages written.

   c. An insecure social scientist may respond by engaging in activities which make him appear busy but which are detrimental to long-term evaluation objectives.

8. Status ambiguities strain relationships.

   a. The social scientist may bring to the situation an academic disrespect for practical problems.

   b. Administrators and practitioners, in turn, may be defensive about their educational inferiority and highly sensitive to what they interpret as snobbism on the part of researchers/evaluators.

9. Action agencies nearly always operate on tight budgets with requests for evaluation suffering since often the contribution of research is intangible and uncertain.

10. Publication of results are often controlled since negative reports may threaten public image and access to funds.

11. Publication credits are viewed as property of the researcher/evaluator who contributed the design, data analysis, and write-up, or as property of the administrator who believes he deserves major recognition for conceiving and implementing the program.

C. UTILIZATION OF RESULTS

1. Evaluation research often cannot produce results early enough to be a major factor in short-term policy decisions. Mann (1969) reflected: "The better the study, the longer it takes, and consequently the less usefulness it may have. Conversely, the sloppier the procedures, the more likely it is to provide information of doubtful validity."

2. Evaluators lack authority; they act as advisers, and policy makers are under no obligation to accept their recommendations.

3. Non-use of evaluation findings is sometimes explained by the fact that evaluation was included for the "wrong reasons".

   a. Downs (1965) pointed out that the professional advice is sometimes sought to justify decisions already made or to postpone action.

   b. An evaluation component is sometimes supported because it lends an aura of respectability and prestige to an action enterprise.

   c. Administrators hope evaluators will provide other services, such as the organization of information to justify grant requests.

4. Evaluation may be looked upon as an imposition, something required by law or by the funding agency.

5. Sadofsky (1966) maintains that problems of acceptance and utilization of evaluation findings arise because of:

   a. Discrepancies between the findings of evaluative research and findings produced by informal evaluations.

   b. Differences between the findings of evaluative research and the personal convictions and professional ideologies of decision makers.

   c. Adverse judgments by administrators relative to the competence of evaluators.

6. Administrators sometimes discount findings by claiming that the real goals of the project were not measured.

   a. Schulberg and Baker (1968) question the wisdom of building evaluation on the public goals of an organization.

   b. If the administrator is less concerned with the attainment of such publicity stated goals than with his acceptance as a good administrator, the evaluator misreads the administrator's real intent.

D. METHODOLOGICAL CONSIDERATION: MEASUREMENT

1. A basic step in evaluation is the identification of objectives and their measurement. Suchman (1966) suggests that formulated objectives have five aspects:

   a. Content of the objective; i.e., the social conditions or behavior patterns to be changed by the program.

   b. Target of the program; i.e., the population to which the program is addressed.

   c. Time within which the change is to take place.

   d. Number of objectives if they are multiple.

   e. Extent of expect effect.

2. Many evaluators (Freeman, 1965; Suchman, 1967; Greenberg, 1968;

and Weiss, 1966) urge a distinction among immediate, intermediate, and ultimate objectives.

    a. Measurements focusing on immediate and intermediate objectives are particularly important when evaluation results are needed before ultimate objectives can be realized.

    b. When programs fail to realize ultimate objectives, utilization of a hierarchy of objectives may also be useful in accounting for such lack of or limited success.

3. Because the realities of program operations are often inconsistent with public project descriptions, measurement of program inputs has also been recommended (Stake, 1967; Stufflebeam, 1969).

4. Coleman (1969) urged a distinction between resources allocated by organizations and services actually received by clients.

5. It is also desirable to anticipate and measure possible unintended effects of programs including those which are undesirable.

6. Data drawn from agency records may reflect the organizational, professional, and individual interests of those who maintain such records as much as they reflect the behavior which they are supposed to measure.

7. The gathering of additional data to supplement/replace suspect data:

    a. May raise the cost of evaluation.

    b. May lengthen the time of the program and, hence, the evaluation.

    c. May enhance client awareness of the program, thereby adding artificially to its apparent or actual effectiveness.

8. Evaluators suggest the use of unobtrusive measures to offset Hawthorne and/or halo effects.

9. The use of direct behavioral measures rather than attitudinal measures poses fewer validity problems and has more appeal to policy makers and their publics.

10. Timing of measurement is a serious issue:

    a. It is often not clear how soon program effects can be expected.

    b. The stability and durability of changes brought about by programs may also be in doubt.

    c. Ideally, continuous and/or longitudinal studies are suggested.

E. METHODOLOGICAL CONSIDERATIONS: DESIGN

1. To assure that changes in measured behavior can be attributed exclusively to the program at hand, evaluative researchers prefer to employ some form of an experimental design.

2. Random assignment of subjects to control and experimental groups is desirable, but presents problems:

   a. Service orientation: administrators, practitioners, and client representatives are reluctant to allow services to be withheld from those who might benefit from them.

   b. Self-selection: it is difficult to refuse service to those who seek it or provide service to those who resist it.

   c. Innovative practices may spread to and contaminate control groups.

3. Communitywide programs have the added problem of finding truly equivalent groups. Adjustments in design may help:

   a. Match participants with non-participants through the use of covariance.

   b. Time-series designs in which the treatment group is used as its own control through repeated measurements of outcome variables beginning well before program implementation.

   c. By considering others of the experimental and quasi-experimental designs suggested by Campbell and Stanley (1963).

4. Instead of a control group, use a comparison group which receives an alternative treatment (not a placebo treatment).

5. The separation of effects of program content from effects of practitioners' characteristics is another problem.

   a. This is particularly difficult when the number of practitioners is small—staff enthusiasm and confidence may be critical variables.

   b. Use of Rosenthal's (1966) techniques as well as special training and supervision of practitioners may help control experimenter expectancy effects.

6. Program participants are subject to the Hawthorne effect based on their feelings of self-importance as persons selected for special attention and/or the placebo effect based on their faith in the program.

   a. Scriven (1969) calls for multiple experimental groups in order to identify and separate these effects.

   b. Trow (1967) points out that some administrators may try to capitalize on Hawthorne effects by attempting to build an experimental climate into their normal programs.

   c. Sommer (1968) argues that the Hawthorne effect is not an extraneous disruptive influence; rather, it is an ever-present and important factor in any field situation.

7. Novelty, special attention, enthusiasm, program modification, lack of control over participants in large-scale programs, inability to determine whether new programs are supplements to rather than substitutes for

earlier programs, all suggest a combination of rigorous experimental data along with a natural history (observation, etc.) account of events and participants before, during, and after program implementation.

REFERENCES

Campbell, D. T. "Reforms as Experiments," *American Psychologist,* 1969, 24, 409-429.

Campbell, D. T. and Stanley, J. C. *Experiments and Quasi-Experimental Designs for Research on Teaching.* Chicago, IL: Rand McNally, 1966.

Coleman, J. S. "Evaluating Educational Programs: A Symposium," *The Urban Review,* 1969, 3 (4), 6-8.

Downs, A. "Some Thoughts on Giving People Economic Advice," *American Behavioral Scientist,* 1965, 9 (1), 30-32.

Freeman, H. E. and Sherwood, C. "Research in Large Scale Intervention Programs," *Journal of Social Issues,* 1965, 21, 11-28.

Greenberg, B. G. "Evaluation of Social Programs," *Review of the International Statistical Institute,* 1968, 36, 260-277.

Horowitz, I. "The Academy and the Polity: Interaction Between Social Scientists and Federal Administrators," *Journal of Applied Behavioral Science,* 1969, 5, 309-335.

Mann, J. "Evaluating Educational Programs: A Symposium," *The Urban Review,* 1969, 3 (4), 12-13.

Rosenthal, R. *Experimenter Effects in Behavioral Research.* New York, NY: Appleton-Century-Crofts, 1966.

Rossi, P. "Evaluating Social Action Programs," *Trans-action,* 1967, 4, 51-3.

Rossi, P. "Evaluating Educational Programs: A Symposium," *The Urban Review,* 1969, 3 (4), 17-18.

Sadofsky, S. "Utilization of Evaluation Results: Feedback into the Action Program," in J. Shmelzed (Ed.), *Learning in Action.* Washington: U. S. Government Printing Office, 1966.

Schulberg, H. and Baker, F. "Program Evaluation Models and the Implementation of Research Findings," *American Journal of Public Health,* 1968, 58, 1248-1255.

Scriven, M. *The Methodology of Evaluation.* AERA Monograph Series on Curriculum, No. 1, Perspectives of Curriculum Evaluation, 1967.

Scriven, M. "Evaluating Educational Programs: A Symposium," *The Urban Review,* 1969, 3 (4), 20-22.

STANDARDS AND ETHICS

At a recent open forum of educators, a committee (called the Joint Committee on Standards for Educational Evaluation, and chaired by Daniel L. Stufflebeam, and composed of representatives from AERA, APA, NCME, APGA, AASA, ECS, ASCD, AFT, NAEP, NEA, and NSBA—this is a test to see how many acronyms you can recognize!) developed a set of preliminary guidelines which are currently being reviewed by prominent educational evaluators. The committee has tried to note promising practices and pitfalls in evaluation and to develop guidelines that allow for creativity and innovation while maintaining quality standards. These standards will aid in bringing uniformity of practice to the profession.

In similar manner, numerous distinguished evaluators are working or have worked on statements of ethics for evaluators. After three rounds of a Delphi procedure, evaluators (under the auspices of AERA) developed a set of eleven categories that are considered quite representative of the concerns voiced by evaluators as a group.

A short summary statement of the principal areas of the above described efforts are listed below.

I. Standards

A. Utility Standards

1. Audience Identification
2. Evaluator Credibility
3. Information Scope and Selection
4. Valuational Interpretation
5. Report Clarity
6. Report Dissemination
7. Report Timeliness
8. Evaluation Impact

B. Feasibility Standards

   1. Practical Procedures
   2. Political Viability
   3. Cost Effectiveness

C. Propriety Standards

   1. Formal Obligation
   2. Conflict of Interest
   3. Full and Frank Disclosure
   4. Public's Right to Know
   5. Rights of Human Subjects
   6. Human Interactions
   7. Balanced Reporting
   8. Fiscal Responsibility

D. Accuracy Standards

   1. Object Identification
   2. Context Analysis
   3. Described Purposes and Procedures
   4. Defensible Information Sources
   5. Valid Measurement
   6. Reliable Measurement
   7. Systematic Data Control
   8. Analysis of Quantitative Information
   9. Analysis of Qualitative Information
  10. Justified Conclusions
  11. Objective Reporting

II. Ethics

A. General Autonomy of Evaluators

1. Evaluators should be independent to the extent that they can follow professional and personal standards.

2. A client-professional relationship should exist where each can have due respect for the other, but separate responsibilities.

3. Evaluators should be accountable to their clients, but not subordinate to them.

C. Political Realities and Social Contexts

1. Political and social contexts exist and should be duly considered when reporting findings.

2. The true outcomes of the studies should be reported regardless of other factors.

D. Values of the Evaluator

1. Evaluator values may be expressed in the report, but should be identified clearly as personal judgments.

2. Values and personal biases of the evaluator should be made known to the client.

E. Selection of the Design and Methodology

1. The evaluator has the primary responsibility for design and methodology and should make the final decision on them.

2. The design and methodology should be agreed upon by the user before attempted implementation.

F. Letting Others Review the Evaluation Design

1. Review of the design, instrumentation, and other aspects of the evaluation by the client and fellow professionals should be sought.

G. Honest Expression of Limitations and/or Constraints

1. It is an essential responsibility of the evaluator to be honest in reporting limitations and/or constraints of the evaluation.

H. Negative Findings

1. Negative findings should be treated the same as positive findings when reporting to the client.

I. Dissemination of Results

1. Release of results should be dependent upon the terms of the contract between the evaluator and client.

J. Protection Against Invasion of Privacy of Subjects

1. The names of individual subjects should be kept confidential at all times, in accordance with Federal law.

2. The protection (bodily, personal, intellectual, moral, spiritual) of human subjects involved in the data-gathering process should take pre-eminence in design and methodology.

K. Refusal of Evaluation Contract

1. The evaluator should not accept an evaluation contract when evaluator ethics and bias are at stake.

2. The evaluator should not accept an evaluation contract when the task or assignment is clearly beyond his/her scope of expertise.

REFERENCES

Joint Committee on Standards for Educational Evaluation. *Standards for Evaluations of Educational Programs, Projects, and Materials.* New York: McGraw-Hill Book Company, 1981.

Schnee, R. G. "Ethical Standards for Evaluators," *CEDR Quarterly,* 10, 1 (Spring 1977), 2-9.

Stenner, A. J. and Webster, W. B. *Educational Program Audit Handbook.* Arlington, VA: The Institute for the Development of Educational Auditing, 1971.

ESSENTIAL TASKS AND COMPETENCIES IN RESEARCH AND EVALUATION

Training programs to produce evaluation theorists and consultants should be designed to broaden the base from which educational programs and their problems of implementation are viewed. Such programs should provide task-oriented experiences for personnel who will be gathering useful evaluation information at the local level.

Below are listed some of the many competencies that most evaluators and researchers view as desirable for their profession. Needless to say, one can hardly expect to find all personnel highly skilled in each and every competency listed. Most large-scale evaluations are accomplished through a team approach drawing on the identified competencies of several individuals.

A. **Obtaining information about an area to be researched or a phenomenon to be evaluated.**

1. Knowledge of how formal search procedures can be used to obtain information.

2. Ability to use library research techniques.

3. Ability to use ERIC and other information retrieval systems.

4. Knowledge of how to obtain information through informal means, such as identifying and contacting others working in the same area.

B. **Drawing implications from results of prior research and practice.**

1. Ability to review and evaluate research and research-related reports.

2. Ability to review and evaluate relevant educational practices.

3. Ability to draw correct inferences, conclusions, or generalizations.

4. Ability to synthesize or summarize extant knowledge.

C. Conceptualizing the research problem or defining the object of the evaluation.

  1. Ability to identify and articulate the problem in a research study.

  2. Ability to define precisely the phenomenon to be judged in an evaluation study.

D. Selecting an appropriate inquiry strategy for addressing the research or evaluation problem.

  1. Knowledge of the variety of common inquiry strategies in education (e.g., depiction studies, correlational studies, experimental studies).

  2. Knowledge of inquiry strategies in other disciplines (e.g., philosophical analysis, historiography).

E. Formulating hypotheses or questions to be answered by the study.

  1. Ability to formulate testable hypotheses or answerable questions in a research or evaluation study.

  2. Eliciting evaluative questions from all important audiences for the evaluation.

F. Specifying data or evidence necessary for a rigorous test of the hypothesis or an unequivocal answer to the research or evaluation question.

G. Selecting appropriate research and evaluation designs to collect data to test the hypothesis or answer the question.

  1. Knowledge of types of designs (e.g., experimental, quasi-experimental, naturalistic).

  2. Knowledge of the questions which can and cannot be answered by each design.

  3. Knowledge of feasibility constraints (e.g., time, access to subjects, control, money) which are associated with each design.

H. Identifying the population to which results should be generalized, and selecting a sample of the populations.

  1. Ability to identify the population of concern.

  2. Ability to differentiate between theoretical populations and accessible populations.

  3. Knowledge of sampling theory and techniques, including variations on simple random sampling such as stratified sampling, cluster sampling, and multi-stage sampling.

I. **Applying the research or evaluation design and recognizing or controlling threats to validity.**

   1. Ability to recognize and eliminate or account for threats to validity inherent in any design under use.

   (For Experimental or Quasi-Experimental Studies)

   2. Knowledge of specific experimental and quasi-experimental research designs.

   3. Knowledge of factors which jeopardize internal and external validity.

   4. Ability to design studies to control extraneous variables.

   5. Knowledge of randomization as a means of experimental control and its relationship to inferential statistics.

   6. Knowledge of fixed-effects, random-effects, and mixed-effects designs; crossed and nested factors; the nature of interactions and their graphing and interpretation.

   7. Knowledge of covarying, blocking, and stratifying as means of increasing precision of estimation in experimental designs.

   8. Knowledge of the effect of measurement error on the precision (power) of an experiment.

   9. Knowledge of purposes underlying the use of randomized blocks, Latin square, fractional factorial, incomplete block designs, etc.

J. **Identifying at appropriate levels of generality the goals of the program to be evaluated.**

   1. Ability to identify all audiences which should help determine program goals.

   2. Ability to help others identify their goals.

   3. Ability to help others prioritize their goals.

K. **Assessing the value and feasibility of program goals.**

   1. Ability to determine appropriate standards for judging program goals.

   2. Ability to apply standards to program goals to determine the worth of those goals.

   3. Ability to determine the feasibility of program goals in relation to resources available to try to attain those goals.

   4. Ability to determine actual and intended system outcomes to identify discrepancies (needs) which exist in the system.

L. **Translating broad objectives into specific (measurable) objectives.**

   1. Ability to state objectives in measurable terms.

   2. Ability to elicit and incorporate reactions of program personnel to statements of specific objectives.

M. Identifying standards or norms for judging worth.

N. Monitoring the program to detect deviations from design or specified procedures.

O. Identifying classes of variables for measurement.

P. Selecting or developing techniques of measurement.

   1. Knowledge of properties of nominal, ordinal, interval, and measurement scales.

   2. Knowledge of fundamental theorems on the differential weighting of test items.

   3. Knowledge of general principles of instrument construction.

   4. Knowledge of major forms of assessment of knowledge and cognitive skills including multiple-choice, completion, free-response, ranking, matching formats, etc.

   5. Knowledge of primary methods of assessing attitudes and other affective variables, including Likert and Thurstone scales, semantic differential, Q-sort, sociometry, etc.

   6. Knowledge of how to construct and use rating scales (including methods of assessing rater agreement), checklists, questionnaires, interview schedules, and observation systems.

   7. Ability to write unambiguous items and in vocabulary appropriate to the specified audience.

   8. Ability to select appropriate standardized tests or instruments.

   9. Knowledge of uses of criterion-referenced and objectives-referenced testing.

Q. Assessing the validity of measurement techniques.

   1. Fundamental postulates and theorems of classical true-score theory.

   2. Knowledge of or ability to determine instrument reliability, including types of reliability coefficients.

   3. Knowledge of or ability to determine instrument validity, including various approaches to determining validity.

   4. Knowledge of norming procedures.

.5. Ability to conduct item analyses, including computing difficulty and discrimination indices.

R. Using appropriate methods to collect data (tests, interviews, etc.).

1. Ability to administer all data collection instruments necessary to one's research or evaluation study.

2. Ability to conduct all necessary "non-instrument" data collection techniques, such as interviews and content analysis.

S. Choosing and employing appropriate techniques of statistical analysis.

1. Knowledge of the general roles of statistical techniques (e.g., descriptive vs. inferential use of statistics).

2. Knowledge of differences in major classes of statistical techniques (e.g., Bayesian vs. Fisherian inference; parametric vs. nonparametric statistics) and principal concepts associated with each class.

3. Knowledge of models and theories underlying statistical techniques (e.g., general linear model, permutation theory, properties of principal probability distributions).

4. Knowledge of major concepts and use of principal statistical techniques (e.g., pqrtial correlation, analysis of covariance).

5. Knowledge of assumptions underlying principal statistical techniques and consequences of failure to meet these assumptions.

6. Ability to choose (or design) appropriate statistical techniques for analysis of a particular set of data.

7. Ability to use specific statistical techniques correctly.

T. Using electronic computers and computer-related equipment.

1. Ability to use computer-related equipment such as sorters, reproducers, or automatic test scoring machines.

2. Ability to design card layouts to allow data analysis within computer constraints, and ability to use standardized computer programs (e.g., BMD series).

3. Ability to write computer programs.

4. Ability to use computer coding.

5. Knowledge of capabilities of local computer systems.

6. Ability to read and interpret computer output.

U. Interpreting and drawing appropriate conclusions from data analysis.

V. Reporting research and evaluation findings and implications.

1. Knowledge of the technical background and experience of the audience(s) for the report.

2. Ability to write in a style and at a level appropriate to a specified audience.

3. Ability to put quantitative or numerical information into verbal or narrative form.

4. Knowledge of alternate methods of presenting statistical data (e.g., charts, graphs, or tables).

5. Knowledge of publication outlets for research reports, articles, or books.

6. Ability to prepare and deliver an oral report of the research of evaluation findings.

W. Making recommendations as a result of the evaluation.

1. Ability to translate data analyses into recommendations for action.

X. Providing immediate feedback on program performance for use in decisions about program modification.

1. Ability to develop techniques for providing evaluative feedback to program or project personnel in time to allow needed modifications to be made during the operation of the program.

2. Ability to identify the decision makers who need evaluative feedback.

Y. Obtaining and managing resources (material and human) necessary to conduct the research or evaluation study.

1. Knowledge of effective techniques for writing and submitting proposals to obtain funding and negotiating with funding agencies.

2. Knowledge of legalities related to research and evaluation projects.

3. Ability to determine human and financial resources necessary to conduct a program or project and use accounting procedures to operate within a program or project budget.

4. Ability to estimate realistically the time required for research and evaluation activities.

5. Knowledge of and ability to use management and planning systems such as PERT (Program Evaluation and Review Techniques), PPBS (Program Planning Budgeting System), or Critical Path Analysis.

REFERENCES

Anderson, R. D., Soptick, J. M., Rogers, W. T., & Worthen, B. R. An Analysis and Interpretation of Tasks and Competencies Required of Personnel Conducting Exemplary Research and Research-Related Activities in Education. Technical Paper No. 23. Boulder, CO: AERA Task Force on Research Training, Laboratory of Educational Research, 1971.

ERIC/TM. *Selecting Educational Researchers and Evaluators.* TM Report 48. Princeton: ERIC/TM.

Worthen, B. R. "Competencies for Educational Research and Evaluation." *Educational Researcher,* 1975, 4, 13-16.

COMPETENCIES AND QUALIFICATIONS FOR RESEARCH IN SCHOOLS

Schools participating in educational research projects are demanding to do just that—participate rather than simply be regarded as experimental units. Participation requires recognition of school personnel as partners rather than subjects in research efforts.

A. **MAKING INITIAL CONTACT WITH SCHOOLS**

1. Ability to determine (Local Education Agency) LEA staff person likely to be most interested in the content of particular project or product.

2. Ability to establish liaison with this LEA staff person and proceed to plan strategy for contacting other LEA staff who will make final decisions.

3. Ability to discuss project requirements with school-level staff person most interested in content of project.

4. Ability to establish liaison with this school-level staff person and proceed to plan strategy for contacting other school staff involved in making final decisions.

B. **CLARIFYING THE PARTICIPATORY ROLE OF SCHOOL STAFF**

1. Ability to talk and listen to LEA and school-level staff regarding aspects of project purpose and design.

2. Ability to offer school or students assurance concerning anonymity and confidentiality.

3. Ability to detect possible dangers to teachers/students.

C. **OPENING AND MAINTAINING A CHANNEL FOR COMMUNICATION WITH LEA AND SCHOOL-LEVEL STAFF**

1. Knowledge of what communication mode is most convenient for LEA and school-level staff.

2. Ability to cover all communication costs pertaining to project.

3. Ability to make LEA, school visits when requested to do so.

D. MEETING(S) WITH LEA, SCHOOL-LEVEL STAFF REGARDING PROPOSED RESEARCH

1. Ability to assess school's willingness to participate.

2. Ability to determine when one or more meetings can be scheduled.

3. Ability to determine who will participate in such meeting(s).

4. Ability to send project materials to all participants.

5. Ability to explain purpose and design of project to all persons at such meeting(s).

6. Ability to stay in on-site area for additional meetings.

7. Ability to maintain flexible data collection procedures and information (or product) dissemination procedures so that LEA, school-level staff suggestions can be incorporated.

8. Knowledge of project aspects that are likely to produce most interesting and beneficial results for all.

9. Ability to explain projected "returns" from project to all involved.

E. SCHEDULING OF DATA COLLECTION

1. Knowledge of what alternative sampling methods can be allowed.

2. Knowledge of the relative problems and merits of each alternative sampling method.

3. Ability to accommodate LEA, school staff recommendations for sampling methods.

4. Ability to change to alternative sampling method, if necessary.

5. Knowledge of what alternative data collection schedules can be followed.

6. Knowledge of the relative problems and merit of each alternative data collection schedule.

7. Ability to accommodate LEA, school staff recommendations for data collection schedule.

8. Ability to change data collection schedule as needed.

F. CONDUCTING ON-SITE RESEARCH

1. Ability to provide sufficient staff to carry out data collection.

2. Ability to include LEA, school staff in data collection.

3. Ability to provide all necessary supplies and materials for data collection.

4. Knowledge of school rules and policies so as to maintain consistency in interaction with staff and students.

G. CONDUCTING FOLLOW-UP ACTIVITIES

1. Ability to provide sufficient staff to carry out all follow-up activities.

2. Ability to work with students individually or in groups.

3. Ability to conduct workshops with LEA, school staff to present results or final report.

4. Ability to remain on site for additional meetings and/or workshops.

H. MAINTAINING OPEN COMMUNICATION CHANNEL

1. Ability to assess overall LEA, school staff interest in project results.

2. Knowledge of what further roles the LEA, school staff would be interested in playing with regard to completed project.

3. Ability to cover all communication costs regarding project follow-up.

4. Ability to provide LEA, school staff with information related to and directly issuing from the project.

REFERENCES

Rossi, R. J. *Educational Researcher,* 4, 8 (September), 1975, 3-4.

UNIT II

PROBLEM SOLVING TECHNIQUES

	Page
BRAINSTORMING	29
DELPHI TECHNIQUE	33
FORCE FIELD ANALYSIS	41
TASK ANALYSIS	45
Q-SORT TECHNIQUE	49
NEEDS ASSESSMENT	53

BRAINSTORMING

The brainstorming technique is a method for eliciting creative ideas to solve a problem. Osborn (1963) defines brainstorming as using the brain to storm a problem. The term also refers to a basic principle—the principle of suspended judgment.

Scientific research has proven that adherence to this principle produces highly productive results in both individual and group efforts. In other words, for the best results, we should turn on our judicial minds at one time and our creative minds at another instead of trying to think both critically and imaginatively at one and the same time. This does not mean that ideas produced do not need to be evaluated, but rather that this should be done at another time.

A. FOUR BASIC RULES

1. Criticism is ruled out. Adverse judgment of ideas must be withheld until later.

2. "Free wheeling" is encouraged. The wilder the idea is, the better; it is easier to tame down than to think up.

3. Quantity is wanted. Quantity breeds quality in idea production.

4. Combination and improvement are sought: shirt-tailing, hitchhiking, piggybacking, etc., on others' ideas is wanted.

B. PRELIMINARY PROCEDURES

1. Panel leader should be trained in advance for his/her function.

2. The problem under consideration should be specific and concise rather than general.

    a. Narrow the problem so that the group members shoot at a single target.

3. "Warm-up" practice exercises should be used.

4. Participants should be given a short background memo at least two days in advance.

    a. The purpose of the memo is to orient the members and to let them sleep on the problem.

5. The ideal group size is about twelve.

6. Assign some self-starters to each group.

C. CONDUCTING THE SESSION

1. Keep the atmosphere informal.

2. Present the four basic rules (see Section A above).

    a. A placard is usually used to display these rules.

3. Adherence to the principle of suspended judgment is essential for success.

4. Explain the problem in own words.

5. Call for suggestions.

    a. Recognize those who raise their hands to signify that they have an idea to offer.

    b. Each presents only one idea at a time.

    c. If someone wishes to combine or "piggyback," he simply snaps his fingers for immediate recognition.

6. Record all ideas.

    a. It is most useful to have a secretary who is not participating in the session.

    b. Ideas written in abbreviated form on a chalkboard can serve continuously to stimulate imaginative thinking.

    c. Tape recording furnishes a complete record for convenience of recall.

7. Limit the time for each session—optimum is about fifteen minutes.

8. Contact the participants the following day to get subsequent suggestions.

D. EVALUATION OF IDEAS

1. The secretary prepares a triple-spaced, typewritten list of all ideas suggested during the session (and possibly from the next day's follow-up).

2. The chairman edits the list, making sure that each idea is succinctly but understandably stated.

3. The list is retyped grouping ideas by categories.

E. EVALUATION SESSION

1. The evaluation can be done by the brainstorming group or by another group.
2. Regardless of which group does the evaluation, the resolution of the problem is still a group responsibility.
3. To facilitate the evaluation process, a checklist of criteria can be used.
   a. Is it feasible?
   b. Is the idea simple enough?
   c. Is it timely?
   d. Is it appropriate?
   e. Is it efficient?
   f. Is it an improvement?

F. ADVANTAGES OF BRAINSTORMING

1. It involves the total group.
2. It has the security of suspended judgment.
3. It produces a variety of approaches to a problem.
4. It produces unique ideas.
5. It can serve to improve morale.
6. It stimulates creativity and imagination.
7. It creates an awareness of dichotomies.

G. DISADVANTAGES OF BRAINSTORMING

1. It can create conflict.
2. It can create a sense of insecurity.
3. It represents an inefficient use of time as compared to autocracy.
4. It can fail if not carefully planned.

REFERENCES

Osborn, A. F. *Applied Imagination.* New York, NY: Charles Scribner's Sons, 1963.

Redefer, F. L. "Magnet for Ideas: Brainstorming in Education," *Saturday Review,* August 8, 1964.

Wood, R. W. "Brainstorming: A Creative Way to Learn," *Education,* November 1970.

DELPHI TECHNIQUE

This technique is a method for the systematic solicitation and collation of expert opinion. It is applicable whenever policies and plans have to be based upon informed judgments. Developed by the Rand Corporation, it assists in the decision-making process, particularly when the best answer is highly uncertain. Originally, it was developed to help make decisions about the future. It has now been used in providing information about desirable educational goals.

A. RATIONALE

1. The democratic method of resolving contradictions among the people was epitomized in 1942 in the formula, "unity, criticism, unity." To elaborate, it means starting from the desire for unity, resolving contradictions through criticism or struggle, and arriving at a new unity on a new basis. In our experience, this is the correct method of resolving contradictions among the people.—Mao Tsetung in *On the Correct Handling of Contradictions Among the People.*

   a. The above form of solution can be traced back to the 5th Century B.C. Greek settlement of Elea.

   b. It appears in the Socratic dialog and in the Hegelian and Marxian dialectic of "thesis, antithesis, synthesis."

2. Social scientists studying organizational behavior have adopted the presumption that while rationality is a desirable basis for choice making, given the nature of man, his organizations, and his contradictory emotions and needs, it is *not* realistic to assume that rationality can become the primary basis of collective choice making.

   a. Hence, organizational behaviorists have adopted the position that decision making in an organization is basically a nonrational process.

3. There is no question but that the configuration of shared values, the structure of roles that set the relationships between individuals in the group, the reward and penalty systems, the mechanisms of social control, the division of labor, and the technology of a group all have considerable impact upon its decision-making processes.

B. DEFINITION AND DIMENSIONS

1. The Delphi Technique is a method for the systematic collection of informed judgments on a particular topic.

2. It involves the collection and use of expert opinion in order to generate an informed consensus about seemingly unresolvable problems.

   a. The consensus would be uncontaminated by specious persuasion, the effects of personal prestige, rank, or charisma, the difficulty of abandoning a publicly expressed opinion, and the pressure to conform to a majority opinion exerted within a group meeting.

3. Committees appointed from the community tend to become groups in which people with axes to grind are most active—the more voluble prevail.

   a. Trending information is difficult to obtain from established committees.

4. Research indicates that the controlled feedback and iteration system tends to produce a convergence of ideas as to what the goals and objectives should be, but it does not lose information as to the divergent goals.

   a. Significant divergent viewpoints will be identified and the school system can develop alternative programs to serve such views.

5. The Delphi Technique, then, is used for pooling expert opinion in situations where objective criteria are not available, and is characterized by three essential features:

   a. Anonymity, which reduces the effect of interpersonal relationships and group dynamics.

   b. Controlled feedback to succeeding questionnaires, which allows participants to review a summary of previous responses and provides a continuous flow of data.

   c. Statistical group response, which reduces group pressure for conformity and ensures that the opinion of every member of the participant group is represented in the final response.

C. THE DELPHI PROCESS

1. Selection of a Delphi panel of experts.

   a. For educational goals, the experts are the people—students, teachers, parents, administrators, minority groups, etc.–who have a perspective on education that will yield useful information.

    b. Include the entire group, if possible; if too large, use randomized stratification sampling techniques.

2. Each panel member is asked to write statements or judgments (five to ten) about the issue under consideration

    a. Such opinions are given anonymously and without benefit of consultation with other participants.

    b. All responses are collected and clustered into groups with other statements that have a close relationship.

    c. This collecting and combining takes place without acknowledgement of individual authorship.

    d. No individual statement is dropped.

    e. For convenience, a name is given to each cluster.

3. A complete set of these statements is returned to each panel member for further consideration.

    a. Participants are asked to rewrite their opinion on the basis of the new knowledge contributed by other experts.

    b. Reasons for judgments can be solicited (anonymously) and sent to the entire panel for their consideration.

4. There is no effort to force consensus; the objective is rather to identify and retain all shades of judgments about the issue and to rank the judgments in order of relative importance.

5. This process is repeated until a consensus (or near consensus) is reached.

    a. The Delphi procedures are cumulative.

D. ROUNDS

1. Each questionnaire dissemination and analysis is termed a *round*.

    a. Typically, a Delphi can be planned to last three or four rounds spaced at approximately six-week intervals.

2. The *first round* is largely exploratory and designed to open up new areas of thought.

    a. The panel is asked to respond individually to a questionnaire and to make independent judgments about the issue(s) in question.

    b. This first questionnaire may contain open-ended questions.

    c. This first round questioning might be considered a needs assessment relative to the issue at hand.

3. *Round two* consists of a second questionnaire developed from an

analysis of the first questionnaire.

   a. It is sent to the same panel of respondents.

   b. It may contain both the items about which opinions are desired as well as a statistical summary (median, interquartile range) of the distribution of responses previously obtained.

   c. Each panel member is now asked to reconsider his previous set of answers.

   d. In particular, a percentage of respondents who gave the most extreme individual forecasts on the preceding round (usually the upper and lower quartiles) are asked to reconsider their answers in light of their deviance from the group norm.

   e. If a panel member should decide to revise his response, and/or if his new response falls outside the interquartile range provided from all other respondents' answers, he is asked to explain the rationale for his response.

4. The questionnaire used in *round three* contains a summary of previous responses given in statistical terms.

   a. In addition, the full panel is given short summaries of the reasons reported by those panel members whose responses differed from the majority opinion.

   b. As before, respondents are invited to revise their responses and, if these answers are still outside the second round interquartile range, to summarize the rationale that supports their position.

5. As the second and third rounds progress, the areas of interest are narrowed and group views on certain topics begin to emerge.

6. By the *fourth round,* there is a clear indication of the group's opinions and attitudes on the issue(s).

7. Throughout the rounds, respondents are encouraged to formulate new questions and explore new alternatives besides thinking deeply about the questions asked.

8. Whenever a consensus of judgment is obtained on an issue, it is usually dropped from further exploration in succeeding questionnaires.

9. Whenever polarization of views occurs, an attempt is made to develop questions designed to highlight reasons for this polarization.

   a. The degree to which the design team chooses to explore a majority-minority type polarization will be a stronger function of the arguments or comments made than of the actual number of individuals taking a particular view.

10. Statistical group response defines the group response (median or mean) but permits the retention of divergent judgments.

11. Iteration (controlled feedback) has the effect of closing the spread of answers.

    a. Individual opinions tend to converge but do not come to a single point.

12. At the conclusion of the rounds, various analyses can be conducted based upon perceptions of subpopulations within the panel.

E. UTILIZATION OF THE DELPHI TECHNIQUE

1. A common thread underlying the appropriateness for utilizing the Delphi technique is related to the following properties:

    a. The issue(s) under consideration does not lend itself to precise analytical techniques but can benefit from subjective judgments on a collective basis.

    b. The individuals needed to contribute to the examination of complex or broad issues have no history of adequate communication and may represent diverse backgrounds with respect to experience or expertise.

    c. More individuals are needed than can effectively interact in a face-to-face exchange.

    d. Time and cost factors make frequent group meeting impractical.

    e. The efficiency of face-to-face meetings can be increased by a supplemental group communication process.

    f. Disagreements among individuals are so severe or politically unpalatable that the communication process must be refereed and/or anonymity assured.

    g. The heterogeneity of the participants must be preserved to assure validity of results; i.e., avoidance of domination by quantity or by strength of personality ("bandwagon effect").

F. ASSUMPTIONS OF THE TECHNIQUE

1. Participant variables: critical to the validity and reliability of the Delphi are a number of characteristics of the panel members.

    a. Representativeness of the panel: a sufficient number to ensure that the outcome accurately represents thinking in the field.

    b. Appropriateness and competence of the panel: each has been appropriately chosen and is competent to render the judgments required.

    c. Commitment of panel: members will give carefully considered judgments to repeated questionnaires.

    d. Clarity of questionnaire: panel respondents will understand the questionnaire items.

    e. Independence of responses: responses will not be affected by statistical reporting of other responses as they would by pressures of a convened group.

    f. Personality differences of panel: individual dispositional differences will not affect response patterns.

    g. Nonrespondents: there is no significant difference between respondents and those who fail to complete and return the survey instruments.

2. Procedural variables: the designer of a Delphi study should consider the following:

    a. Pertinent items: item content in the first round questionnaire generates information germane to the study.

    b. Interval between rounds: the amount of delay between iterations does not affect individual estimations.

    c. Method of reporting previous responses: the manner of aggregating the previous expert opinions does not affect later responses.

    d. Number of questionnaires: the number of rounds does not affect the result.

    e. Questionnaire format: the initial questionnaire might be open ended or require specified responses.

3. Outcomes: the technique assumes that the following is probable.

    a. Consensus represents a high probability of an accurate forecast.

    b. Recognized experts in a field are good predictors.

    c. Anonymity is a valuable feature of the technique; although responses are anonymous, participation on the panel is not necessarily anonymous.

G. DELPHI CAVEATS

1. Imposing monitor views and preconceptions of a problem upon the respondent group by over-specifying the structure of the Delphi and not allowing for the contribution of other perspectives related to the problem.

2. Assuming that the Delphi can be a surrogate for all other human communications in a given situation.

3. Poor techniques of summarizing and presenting the group response and ensuring common interpretations of the evaluation scales used in the exercise.

4. Ignoring and not exploring disagreements so that discouraged dissenters drop out and an artificial consensus is generated.

5. Understanding the demanding nature of a Delphi and the fact that the respondents should be recognized as consultants and properly compensated for their time if the Delphi is not an integral part of their job function.

Examples of The Delphi Technique

A. *EDUCATIONAL GOAL INDEX* (PRELIMINARY)

1. Each panel member is asked to write what he considers to be five to ten important goals of education.

2. These are collected and combined into one list.

3. Similar ideas are grouped into clusters (approximately ten major categories), and are given labels or titles.

4. These clustered groups bearing labels are then distributed to the respondents in a second round.

5. The respondents are asked to rate the clusters in order of importance, using a scale of 0-100.

6. Following this round, the median response was computed for each goal, with a name given to label the cluster of goal statements.

B. *QUALITY OF LIFE INDEX*

1. Each panel member is now asked to identify factors they believed produced a "Quality Life," that made life worthwhile.

2. Follow steps two through six above. (The purpose of clustering is to keep the number of items manageable; a group of 150 people can easily generate 600 to 800 statements in the first round.)

C. *EDUCATION GOAL INDEX*

1. The first and second rounds produced a preliminary list of goal statements ranked in order of importance.

2. The next rounds produced a ranked list of "Quality of Life" factors.

3. The panel is now asked to rate the goals of education in terms of their contribution to the "Quality of Life" factors. This furnishes a quantitive index of the relevance of education to the quality of life of the individual.

4. This new look at the goals invariably results in different rankings.

D. *PERCEIVED ACHIEVEMENT INDEX*

1. This new list is given to the panel who are asked to evaluate how well they thought their school(s) was doing in progressing towards these goals.

E. *PRIORITY INDEX*

1. When rankings for goal importance are compared with those for school achievement, a priority index results. Since the same 0-100 scale has been used, direct comparisons are possible.

2. The discrepancy between goal importance and perceived goal achievement produces a numerical value of the need for improvement; the greater the discrepancy, the higher the priority.

REFERENCES

Arnfield, R. V. (Ed.). *Technological Forecasting.* Chicago, IL: Aldine Publishing Company, 1969.

Center for Futures Research. *Annual Report 1976 and Five-Year Review, 1971-76.* Los Angeles, CA: University of Southern California Graduate School of Business Administration, 1976.

Dalkey, N. C., et al. *The Delphi Method: An Experimental Study of Group Opinion.* Santa Monica, CA: The Rand Corporation, 1972.

Helmer, O. *Systematic Use of Expert Opinions.* Santa Monica, CA: The Rand Corporation, 1967.

Hencley, S. P. and Yates, J. R. *Futurism in Education.* Berkeley, CA: McCutchan Publishing Corporation, 1974.

Linstone, H. A. and Turoff, M. (Eds.). *The Delphi Method: Techniques and Application.* Boston, MA: Addison-Wesley Publishing Company, 1973.

Rasp, A. "Delphi: A Decision-maker's Dream," *Nation's Schools,* 92:1 (July 1973), 29-32.

Sackman, H. *Delphi Technique.* Lexington, MA: D. C. Health and Company, 1975.

FORCE FIELD ANALYSIS

Force field analysis, sometimes referred to as context analysis, is a process for analyzing the context of issues under observation and the forces which help or hinder in meeting goals related to the issues. It involves first clarifying what the selected issues mean and then restating each as a *goal*. This step is important because an issue is a statement of the situation as it presently exists, whereas a goal is a statement of how we would like the situation to exist at some future time. Perceived discrepancies between what exists now and what is desired lie at the heart of context analysis.

After goals are stated, the current situation is assessed by delineating the forces *for* and *against* movement toward each goal. The present situation exists because we are in a sort of balance or equilibrium determined by these forces (see figure below). If we increase the forces which push toward the goal and/or decrease the forces pushing away from the goal, we will move toward the goal. Thus, the major problem in reaching the goal will be to change the forces. But, before planning this, we must clearly understand what each is and how it operates.

Figure 1
CONTEXT ANALYSIS

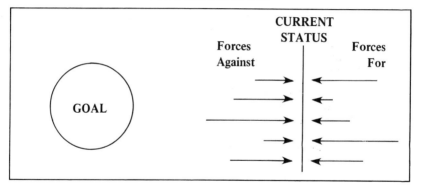

A. **FORCE FIELD ANALYSIS**

   1. Clarify what the selected issues mean and restate each as a goal.

   2. Identify discrepancies between what is and what is desired (goal).

   3. Assess the current situation by delineating the forces *for* and those *against* movement toward the goal.

   4. After the forces are delineated for each goal (or issue), judgments are made as to the:

      a. *Clarity* of each force.

      b. *Strength* of each force.

      c. *Resistance to change* of each force.

   5. *Clarity* refers to the ability to describe the force in understandable terms to someone who has not been a party to the discussion.

   6. The reason for making judgments relative to *strength* and *resistance to change* is to lay a basis for determining the strategies to adopt in attempting to change the forces.

B. **STRATEGIES**

   1. Other things being equal, the best strategy is to concentrate on forces which are less *resistant to change*.

      a. For example, my goal may be to increase the audience of an educational television station, but a strong force against it may be a commitment to culturally sophisticated programming.

      b. The above may be easy or difficult to change, depending on the views of the station's policy-making group.

   2. It may be, in some cases, of course, better to concentrate on a *very strong* force which is *resistant to change* rather than on several weaker ones which are easy to change.

      a. For example, putting through a bond issue in these difficult times may be the best way to solve a facilities problem, in spite of the fact that a lot of stopgap measures could be taken.

      b. Conversely, it would be a waste of time and effort to concentrate on a force which was impossible to change.

C. **SMALL GROUP SESSIONS**

   1. Participants are divided into several small groups, with each group concentrating on a different issue.

   2. Each group initially goes through the total process of:
      a. Changing the issue into a goal statement.
      b. Identifying the forces.

      c. Making judgments relative to them.

3. Hopefully, there will be enough small groups (dyads—two persons—are excellent here) so that each issue can be worked on by two groups.

4. These two separate groups work on an issue and then join and resolve their differences.

5. At an open session, each of the "joined" groups reports to the whole, and the decisions reached are discussed.

6. The groups then break again and revise their work.

D. STRATEGY SELECTION

1. Strategy selection involves selecting general strategies which, for each goal or issue, are designed to:

      a. Strengthen forces for.

      b. Weaken forces against.

      c. Accomplish both.

2. The underlying objective is movement toward achievement of the goal.

3. The small group procedures described above should be followed.

      a. Each goal will be handled by separate small groups.

      b. These groups will join, resolve their differences, and report to the total group.

      c. Using feedback from the total group, the small groups will then revise their work.

4. The entire process may last several days (or meetings).

5. At a general final meeting, reports are given by each working subgroup and the results of the complete session are reviewed and summarized.

REFERENCES

Fox, R. S., Schmuck, R., Van Egmond, E., Ritvo, M., and Jung, C. *Diagnosing Professional Climate of Schools.* NTL Learning Resources Corporation, Inc., Fairfax, VA, 1973.

TASK ANALYSIS

Task analysis techniques are involved primarily with the prescription of the prerequisites and conditions under which behaviors may be developed and a description of the behaviors which constitute a given performance.

Task analysis is not clearly evaluative since the judging process is not involved, but task analysis (like objectives writing) is often a function assigned to the evaluator by his clients.

A. **STEPS IN TASK ANALYSIS**

    1. Specify the main task or performance.

        a. This statement should indicate what the subject is to do upon the use of a given product and the situation in which he is to perform.

    2. Identify subtasks.

        a. These statements should include the skills that the subject must possess in order to demonstrate the criterion performance.

    3. For each subtask, identify sub-subtasks which contribute to that subtask.

    4. Terminate reduction of tasks into subtasks when the subtasks are equivalent to the subject's entry behavior.

B. **BASES FOR TASK ANALYSIS**

    1. Task analysis based on objectives.

        a. This method includes the specification of instructional objectives and the specification, for each objective, of the type of behavior (e.g., knowledge, comprehension, receiving, responding, etc.) required for each.

    2. Task analysis based on behavioral analysis (see above example).

3. Task analysis based on information processing.

   a. This method includes a prescription of information to be processed for the performance to be mastered.

   b. Consideration of cues, manipulations to be made, feedback, etc., are central to this method.

4. Task analysis based on a decision paradigm.

   a. Underlying decisions which must be made to perform a given task are analyzed and decision chains and procedures are provided.

5. Task analysis based on content structure.

   a. This method includes the identification of rules and examples involved in the task, the presentation of these rules and examples, and the discussion of relationships between/among them.

6. Task analysis based on vocational schemes.

   a. This method involves the reduction of a performance into jobs, duties, tasks, and task elements.

N.B. These categories are not mutually exclusive, but rather do suggest central elements of different approaches to task analysis.

C. PRECAUTIONS

1. The rule of skepticism: No one knows how to do it.

   a. Unless the idea is to subsidize employment of social scientists, the burden of proof should be on the proposer.

2. The rule of delay: If it works at all, it won't work soon.

   a. Be prepared to give the program years.

   b. The three R's of innovation: Risks, Responsibility, Resources.

3. The rule of complexity: Nothing complicated works.

   a. When a new information system contains more variables than, shall we say, the average age of the officials who are to use it, the chances of failure are very high.

4. The rule of thumb: If the data are thicker than your thumb, they are likely to be incomprehensible.

5. The rule of curiosity: Ask many questions.

   a. Unless you understand precisely who will use the data, how often, and at what cost, don't proceed.

6. The rule of length and width: The longer the sequence of steps and the wider the band of clientele, the less likely the information will be useful.

7. The rule of anticipated anguish: Most of the things that can go wrong, will.

TASK ANALYSIS – A LEARNING HIERARCHY
FOR A BASIC READING SKILL

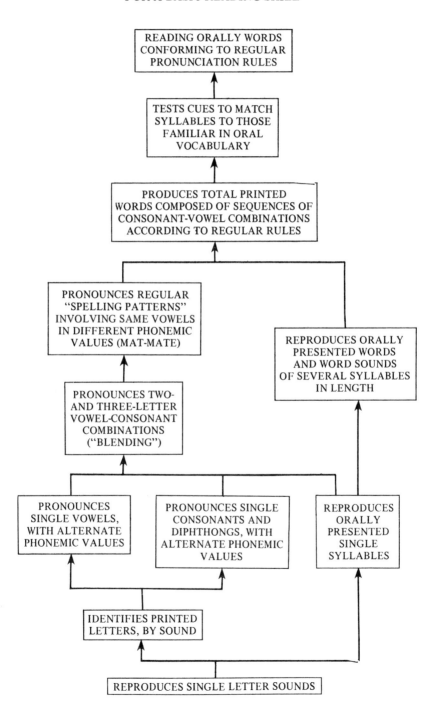

   a. If you do not have substantial reserves of money, personnel, and time to repair breakdowns, do not start.

8. The rule of the known evil: People have a tendency to fear and resist change, even when it seems good.

9. The rule of the mounting mirage: Hypothetical benefits are readily apparent in the present.

   a. The costs lie in the future.

   b. Hypothetical benefits should outweigh estimated costs by a least ten to one before pursuing a pilgrimage to the promised land.

REFERENCES

Anderson, S. B., Ball, S., and Murphy, R. T. *Encyclopedia of Educational Evaluation.* San Francisco, CA: Jossey-Bass, 1975.

Q–SORT TECHNIQUE

One technique for evaluating needs and objectives frequently mentioned in many recent papers on formative evaluation is the Q-Sort. Methods of collecting appraisal or judgmental data from relevant groups of persons through simply and tersely stated needs or objectives is essential in the formative stage of evaluation.

The procedures developed by W. Stephenson (1953) and labeled Q methodology are most appropriate. The Q technique is the logical operationalization of Stephenson's theoretical Q methodology. Briefly, a list of need statements or goal/objective statements may be assigned numerals, placed on cards, and given to persons to rank order according to some pre-determined rules.

The ordinal data that result from the sorts may then be analyzed to yield a number of useful statistics.

A. BASIC TYPES OF Q-SORT

1. *Structured* Q-Sorts are those that include a set of rules whereby a certain number of cards (representing needs or objectives) must be placed in each of a certain number of piles.

   a. For example, the left-hand piles are for the least valuable needs or objectives, while the right-hand piles might be designated for the most valuable.

   b. Here the sort is forced into a pre-determined distribution, according to some theory.

2. *Unstructured* Q-Sorts are those used where there is no underlying theory, and the participants are asked to merely place the cards into a pre-determined number of piles according to their own perceptions of where they should be placed.

   a. In essence, we are saying, "Let the cards fall where they may."

B. Q-SORT PROCEDURES

1. Place unambiguous needs or objectives statements on cards, one to a card.

   a. Theoretically, at least 75, but no more than 140 times, should be sorted.

2. Shuffle or randomly order the cards and give them to the participants to sort.

   a. The same random approach should be applied to each deck of cards.

3. Sort the cards into some pre-determined distribution.

   a. Usually 7-13 piles of cards are used, but this can be modified depending on the needs of the investigator.

   b. For example, if 80 items were to be sorted into a quasi-normal distribution, the following rules might be set:

      Sort the cards into 9 piles with the number in each pile set as follows:

      4   6   10   12   16   12   10   6   4

      Let the left-most pile represent those needs or objectives deemed most valuable, while the right-most pile represents those considered least valuable.

4. Collect the cards as sorted by the participants and assign ranks to the cards in each pile.

   a. For example, assign the value of "1" to cards in the left-most pile and "9" to cards in the right-most pile.

5. Calculate the desired statistics on the resultant data.

C. USEFUL STATISTICS DERIVED FROM Q-SORT ANALYSIS

1. Consistency or homogeneity of ranking within a group of persons.

   a. This answers the question of how much do people agree on their perceptions of the needs or objectives confronting them.

2. Overall—and subgrouped—rankings or sets of priorities on the list of needs or objectives.

   a. The variance for each need or objective is likewise determined.

3. Differences in ranking profiles among groups of persons.

   a. For example, the analysis might reveal a summary of differences among school board members, teachers, administrators, parents, etc., on the priorities or values each assigns to the list.

4. Clusters of needs or objectives as ranked by a given group(s) of participants.

5. Clusters of persons as they rank needs or objectives.

    a. For example, do Republicans vs. Democrats cluster respectively on their priorities?

6. Similarity of the distribution of rankings by a group of persons to an ideal or criterion distribution.

REFERENCES

Stephenson, William. *The Study of Behavior: Q-Sort Technique and Its Methodology*. Chicago, IL: University of Chicago Press, 1953.

NEEDS ASSESSMENT

The concept of needs assessment is widely used and viewed as an essential tool for decision making at all levels of education. The National Assessment program is an example of a national effort to identify educational needs of American youth. Many states now mandate a needs assessment process of their state departments of education as well as of their many local districts. Educators as a group are turning to this concept for answers to a wide variety of questions.

A. DEFINITION (Kaufman & English, 1975)

1. Needs assessment is a process of defining the desired end of a given sequence of curriculum development.

2. It is a process of making specific what schooling should be about and how it can be evaluated.

3. It is not of itself a curricular innovation; rather, it is a method of determining if innovation is necessary and/or desirable.

4. Needs assessment is an empirical process for defining the outcomes of education.

    a. As such, it becomes a set of criteria by which curricula may be developed and compared.

    b. It would help determine which configuration of people, time, and space produces the types of outcomes desired.

5. As a process, it helps determine the validity of behavioral objectives.

6. It is a process by which a variety of means may be selected and related to each other as integral components of a curriculum.

7. It is a process of identifying gaps between current program and desired results, then acting to reduce these gaps.

a. Identification of discrepancies between what is and what should be.

b. Placing of these discrepancies in priority order, selecting those of highest priority for action.

c. Implementation of a new or redesigning of existing curriculum to reduce discrepancies.

B. DEFINITIONS OF NEED (Stufflebeam, 1977)

1. Discrepancy view: a need is a discrepancy between desired performance and observed or predicted performance.

2. Democratic view: a need is a change desired by a majority of some reference group.

3. Diagnostic view: a need is something whose absence or deficiency proves harmful.

4. Analytic view: a need is the direction in which improvement can be predicted to occur given information about current status.

C. RATIONALE FOR THE NEEDS ASSESSMENT PROCESS

1. Needs assessment is rooted in empiricism.

   a. Reality can be known, understood, and represented in symbolic form.

   b. What is currently undefined can become known and accurately defined.

   c. Reality is not static—the constant redefinition of the goals of education to fulfill shifts in priorities responds to a fluid reality.

   d. Needs assessment can be a process for determining the validity of categories by which people view the universe.

2. Everything that exists can be measured.

   a. Some things can be measured directly.

   b. With other things, one must accept as evidence the approximation of attainment through a listing of "goal indicators."

3. Recipients and supporters of schools should be involved in the determination of their goals and effectiveness.

   a. Aims, goals, outcomes of education can be specific.

   b. A public institution cannot be managed by a few professionals.

   c. Educators cannot allow their own demands for security and domination to override challenges to the viability of schools as they have come to be defined by these professionals.

D. STEPS IN THE NEEDS ASSESSMENT PROCESS (Patterson & Czajkowski, 1976)

1. Develop a plan of action.
   a. Steering committee selection.
   b. Determination of who will be involved.
   c. Anticipation of problems.
   d. Development of the capacities to handle data when gathered.

2. Generate goals.
   a. Use currently available lists as starting point.
   b. Work from needs identified through such means as standardized tests, survey questionnaires, etc.
   c. Goals should be derived from a stated philosophy of education and a clear understanding of its implications.

3. Validate goals.
   a. Validate by investigating the extent to which the community understands the survey instrument.
   b. A mail survey with a follow-up interview would supply the most valuable feedback.

4. Prioritize goals.
   a. Educational goals are ultimately translated into budgetary commitments.
   b. Difficulty of isolating and distinguishing between/among the value of economic understanding, cultural appreciation, physical health, etc., of goals suggests a choice be made of "three" most important, "three" least important goals.
   c. Expect community opposition when prioritization is asked.

5. Translate goals into measurable objectives.
   a. Prepare goal indicators.
   b. Consult commercially developed lists of objectives.
   c. Generate community expectations.
   d. Use professional expertise.
   e. Validate objectives by investigating accuracy of translation from goal to objective and the scope of its coverage.

6. Identify assessment tools and/or evaluative strategies.
   a. Use commercially prepared instruments, if appropriate.
   b. Develop in-house instruments to fit specific needs.
   c. Use professional consultants to assist in the identification and/or preparation of these instruments.

    d. Set criterion levels for groups and tests.

7. Collect data.

    a. Determine what grade levels should be assessed.

    b. Determine whether sampling would suffice or whether to include the entire group in the testing proceedings.

    c. Identify supplementary data that could provide additional insights regarding student performance.

8. Analyze data for discrepancies.

    a. Compare performance against expectancies.

    b. Determine probable reasons for discrepancies.

    c. Evaluate other factors affecting performance.

    d. Reexamine goal expectancies in a realistic manner.

9. Prioritize discrepancies.

    a. Discrepancies should be linked with appropriate goals since the goals have already been ranked.

10. Conduct diagnostic/planning sessions to develop implementation strategies to meet identified needs.

    a. Budget and funding should be included in this post session.

    b. Implement strategies.

    c. Reassess previously identified discrepancies through feedback from new or revised program.

REFERENCES

Kaufman, R. and English, F. *Needs Assessment: A Focus for Curriculum Development.* Washington, D.C.: ASCD (NEA), 1975.

Patterson, J. and Czajkowski, T. "District Needs Assessment: One Avenue to Program Improvement," *Phi Delta Kappan,* December 1976, pp. 327-329.

Russell, D., et al. *Developing a Workable Needs Assessment Process.* Los Angeles, CA: Office of Los Angeles County Superintendent of Schools, 1977.

Stufflebeam, D. *Needs Assessment in Evaluation.* Paper presented at the AERA Evaluation Conference, San Francisco, September 1977.

UNIT III

DATA CLASSIFICATION

	Page
LEVELS OF MEASUREMENT	59
VARIABLES	63
SAMPLING	69
FACTOR ANALYSIS	75

LEVELS OF MEASUREMENT

Levels of measurement, as the name implies from its Latin derivate *scala* meaning "ladder," denotes a degree of progressively sophisticated numeric characteristics. In research and statistics, the rules which govern numbers are categorized into four levels: nominal, ordinal, interval, and ratio. Each of the levels has increasingly rigorous numeric characteristics, and hence, each allows greater flexibility for arithmetic manipulations than its predecessor.

This distinction among levels of measurement is more than academic. The level of measurement indicates what statistical tests are and are not appropriate. Researchers pay much attention to the level of measurement.

A. The **NOMINAL** scale is the simplest level of measurement. It exists when numbers are used simply to classify an object by some specific trait or characteristic.

   Example: If a teacher divides her class into two groups for a spelling bee, the boys versus the girls, she is classifying the students on the nominal level of measurement by sex.

   1. The nominal scale may measure truly discrete phenomena, such as race, sex, or categorical variables measured quantitatively.

   2. Each category on the nominal scale is exclusive and exhaustive; one category cannot flow into another (e.g., voters are categorized as Republicans, Independents, or Democrats; they can be only one).

   3. Nominal scale numbers have no numeric meaning; they cannot be added (e.g., telephone numbers or numbers on a football jersey).

   4. Some statistical tests, such as Chi Square or Contingency Coefficient, may be appropriate for nominal data because they focus on frequencies in the various categories.

B. The **ORDINAL** scale of measurement is exercised when objects are rank ordered on a uniform characteristic or on a combination of criteria.

   Example: If a choral director places singers in a row by height, say, shortest to tallest, the ordinal scale is used. Also, ordinal measurement is used if a teacher ranks students by the combined criteria of test scores and grade point averages.

   1. Ordinal data are typically expressed in terms of highest to lowest, hottest to coldest, best to worst (but not *how* much higher, hotter, or better).

   2. Ordinal numbers indicate rank order and nothing more; the arithmetic operations of addition, subtraction, multiplication, and division are *not* possible.

   3. Ordinal numbers do *not* indicate that the intervals between the numbers are equal (e.g., the difference between the heights of persons, although ranked in height order, may not be the same).

   4. Ordinal numbers do not have an absolute zero point (e.g., if a student gets none right on a ten-word vocabulary test, it does not indicate that there are no words at all that he can spell).

   5. Ordinal scale data require statistical tests that are appropriate for rank order measures: rank order coefficient of correlation, Kendall's W, and rank order analysis of variance, medians, and percentiles.

C. The **INTERVAL** measurement scale exists when objects not only can be ordered but may also be assigned numbers so that equal differences between the numbers reflect equal differences in the amounts of the attribute measured.

   Example: If a scientist measures the temperature on three successive days and finds it to be 68°, 77°, and 59°, the values are interval data; the temperatures can be rank ordered and the differences between one degree and the next higher or lower degree is the same regardless of the starting point (e.g., 1° and 2° are the same distance apart at 99° and 100°).

   1. Interval or *equal-interval* scales possess all the characteristics of nominal and ordinal scales.

   2. Interval scale data can be added or subtracted although these data cannot be multiplied or divided.

   3. The interval scale does not possess a true zero point (e.g., 0° does not mean there is no heat).

   4. It is probable that most educational and psychological tests approximate interval measurement regardless of the fact that most behavioral

sciences measurements do not possess the obvious advantages of physical scales.

5. A myriad of statistical tests are possible by assuming that educational scales (e.g., tests of memory, learning, thinking) are interval.

D. The **RATIO** scale is the highest level of measurement. Numbers on this scale indicate actual amounts of the property being measured.

Example: If a teacher measures the length of a bulletin board, a ratio scale is employed: the differences between measurement units are equal (the same linear distance exists between 2" and 3" as between 9" and 10"), and 0" does mean there is a complete absence of length.

1. Ratio scales possess all the characteristics of nominal, ordinal, and interval scales.

2. The ratio scale has an absolute zero point, and therefore, the arithmetic operations of addition, subtraction, multiplication, and division are possible.

3. Ratio levels of measurement seldom occur in most measures of achievement.

4. Strictly ratio level of measurement of empirical qualities is very rarely required for statistical methods.

REFERENCES

Anderson, N. H. "Scales and Statistics: Parametric and Nonparametic," *Psychological Bulletin,* 58 (April 1961), 305-16.

Anderson, S. B., Ball, S., and Murphy, R. T. *Encyclopedia of Educational Evaluation.* San Francisco, CA: Jossey-Bass Publishers, 1975.

Gardner, P. L. "Scales and Statistics," *Review of Educational Research,* 45 (Winter, 1975), 43-57.

Siegel, S. *Nonparametric Statistics for the Behavioral Sciences.* New York, NY: McGraw-Hill, 1956.

Thorndike, R. L. *Educational Measurement.* (2nd ed.) Washington, D.C.: American Council on Education, 1971.

Tyler, L. E. *Tests and Measurements.* (2nd ed.) Englewood Cliffs, NJ: Prentice-Hall, 1971.

VARIABLES

Variables have been referred to as "the stuff of all empirical investigation." Simply stated, variables are the vehicles for categorizing qualitative or quantitative data. They allow an order to prevail in all behavioral (and specifically educational) research studies and evaluations. However, variables central to program and evaluative concerns do not have universally accepted definitions. They must be operationally defined anew in each research and evaluative undertaking.

Evaluators must carefully observe the nature of each variable utilized, because they often determine the measurement technique and, in turn, the statistical procedures applied to the data.

A. NATURE OF VARIABLES

1. Variables may be defined as a characteristic which can have more than one value.

2. A constant, by contrast, may be a characteristic which can have only one value.

3. Variables are distinguished on the basis of whether they measure or can be classified in whole units (discrete variables) or whether they measure or can be classified in fractional units (continuous).

4. Four types of discrete variables may be identified.

   a. Dichotomous: allow only two gradations of a characteristic.

      (1) True dichotomy: yes/no; dead/alive; present/absent; etc.

      (2) Arbitrary dichotomy: intoxicated/sober; high income/low income; etc.

   b. Limited category: make possible three to six gradations of response, as "Marital status: single, married, divorced, widowed."

   c. Multiple category: permit more than six but fewer than twenty gradations of response, as "Number of school grades completed," "Religious preference," etc.

    d. Infinite category: require at least twenty gradations of response with no upper limit, as Country of birth," "School population," etc.

5. All categories of variables should possess each of the following internal characteristics.

    a. Homogeneity: all categories should bear a logical relationship to the variable under study and to each other; e.g., Eye color: blue, brown, grey, and hazel; but not "near-sighted."

    b. Inclusiveness: the total set of categories should allow for all possible variations and so permit every observation to be classified. Frequently, this is a "Miscellaneous" or "All others" category, but as a rule of thumb, no more than 10 percent of the responses should fall into such a "miscellaneous" classification.

    c. Usefulness: each category should serve a purpose and provide a meaningful dimension to the variable under study. This characteristic guards against excessive proliferation of categories with its overly precise and petty discrimination.

A VARIABLE CLASSIFICATION PLAN

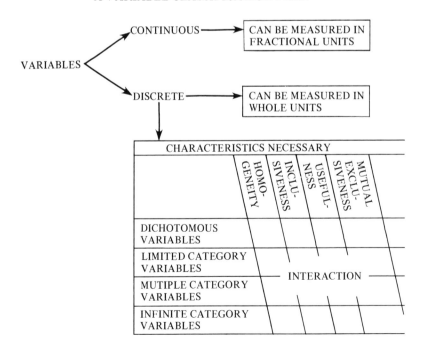

   d. Mutual exclusiveness: each category should represent one unique dimension of the variable under study so that one observation can be classified into one and only one category.

B.   KINDS OF VARIABLES

   Hypothesis: Among students of the same age and intelligence, skill performance is directly related to the number of practice trials, particularly in boys but less directly among girls.

   In the above hypothesis, the variables which must be considered are:

   1. Independent: number of practice trials.
   2. Dependent: skill performance.
   3. Moderator: sex.
   4. Control: age, intelligence.
   5. Intervening: learning.

   1. The *independent* variable is that factor which is manipulated and measured by the researcher to determine a relationship to an observed phenomenon.

      a. It is the variable the researcher will manipulate or change in order to cause a change in some other variable.

      b. It is "independent" in that it is allowed to operate freely so that observations may be made of its effect on another variable.

      c. It is often referred to as the "treatment" variable.

      d. It may be discrete (categorical) and take the form of the presence versus the absence of a particular treatment or approach being studied or a comparison between/among different approaches.

      e. It may be continuous; however, it may be converted to discrete categories by the researchers.

      f. When two continuous variables are compared—as in correlation studies—deciding which variable to call independent and which dependent is sometimes arbitrary. In some cases, the variables are often not labeled since there is no real distinction.

      g. Independent variables may be called *factors* and their variations may be called *levels*.

      Note: Be careful not to confuse an independent variable with two levels for two independent variables.

      E.g., in a study of the effect of music on ability to concentrate, the presence of music (experimental treatment) represents one level of the independent variable, while the absence of music (control) represents another level of the independent variable.

E.g., in a study of the effectiveness of (a) programmed instruction versus (b) instruction by lecture alone versus (c) instruction combining lecture and discussion, there is a single independent variable or factor (type of instruction) with three levels.

2. The *dependent* or *criterion* variable is that factor which is observed and measured to determine the effect of the dependent variable.

   a. It is a response variable or output, representing the consequence of a change in the person or situation being studied.

   b. It is "dependent" because its value will vary according to the manipulation of the independent variable.

   c. Studies may have more than one dependent variable simultaneously.

3. The *moderator* variable is that factor which is measured, manipulated, or selected by the researcher to discover whether it modifies the relationship of the independent variable to an observed phenomenon.

   a. The moderator variable may be thought of as a secondary independent variable.

   b. The word "moderator" simply acknowledges the reason that this secondary independent variable has been singled out for study.

      E.g., when two groups of readers (phonic approach versus sight approach) are tested together, the results of the two methods may appear to be the same; but when fast and slow readers are separated, the two methods may have different results in each subgroup. If so, reading rate (two levels: fast and slow) would seem to *moderate* the relationship between reading approach (independent) and effectiveness (dependent).

   c. Because of the complexity of research situations in the behavioral sciences, the inclusion of at least one moderator variable in a study is highly recommended.

   d. Often the nature of the relationship between two variables remains poorly understood because of the researcher's failure to single out and measure vital moderator variables.

4. The *control* variables are those factors which are controlled by the researcher to cancel out or neutralize any effect they might otherwise have on the observed phenomenon.

   a. All variables in a situation (situational variables) or in a person (dispositional variables) cannot be studied at the same time.

   b. Some must be neutralized to guarantee that they will not have a moderating effect on the relationship between the independent and dependent variables.

c. While the effects of moderator variables are studied, the effects of control variables are neutralized.

d. The effects of control variables can be neutralized by elimination, equating across groups, or randomization.

e. Certain variables appear repeatedly as control variables, although they occasionally serve as moderator variables: sex, intelligence, and socioeconomic status are commonly controlled.

f. The researcher must always decide which variables will be studied (moderator) and which will be neutralized (control).

5. The *intervening* variable is that factor which theoretically affects the observed phenomenon but cannot be seen, measured, or manipulated; its effect must be inferred from the effects of the independent and moderator variables on the observed phenomenon.

E.g., a researcher is going to contrast presenting a lesson on closed-circuit TV versus presenting it via live lecture. His independent variable is mode of presentation; his dependent variable is some measure of learning. He asks himself: "What is it about the two modes of presentation that should lead one to be more effective than the other?" Here he is asking himself what the intervening variable is.

Note: The likely answer—but not certain, since intervening variables are neither visible nor directly measurable—is attention! Closed circuit TV will not present more or less information, but it may stimulate more attention. Thus, the increased attention could consequently lead to better learning.

SCHEMATIC RELATIONSHIP OF THE COMBINED VARIABLES

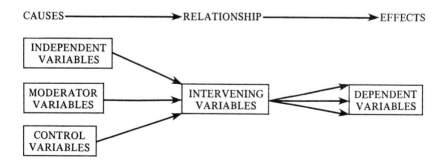

a. We concern ourselves with the identification of intervening variables for the purposes of generalizing.

E.g., in the above example, we must remember that it is the added attention which brings about the results. This added attention can be obtained through other means rather than just closed circuit TV. Researchers must concern themselves with "why" as well as "what" and "how." If attention is the intervening variable, then the researcher must examine attention as a factor affecting learning and use his data as a means of generalizing to other situations and other modes of presentation.

REFERENCES

Fox, D. J. *The Research Process in Education.* New York, NY: Holt, 1969.

Leedy, P. D. *Practical Research: Planning and Design.* New York, NY: Macmillan Publishing Company, 1974.

Suchman, E. A. *Evaluative Research: Principles and Practice in Public Service and Social Action Programs.* New York, NY: Russell Sage Foundation, 1967.

SAMPLING

Sampling refers to the technique of taking any portion of a population as representative of that entire population. It is important to bear in mind that in this definition of sampling, although the sample is *considered* to be representative of a population, it may or may not actually *be* representative. Thus, sampling procedures may be thought of as a kind of quality control. Improving the precision of sampling will result in receiving information more truly reflective of the population under study.

The aim of sampling is to generalize the findings derived from the sample to the larger population from which the sample was selected. Designing a sample to be appropriate for a specific set of circumstances must be done with care, for the kind of sample will determine much of the resulting data.

A. CRITERIA FOR SAMPLE SELECTION.

1. Four considerations are initially required in sample selection.

   a. *Goal orientation* refers to a sampling design being selected which is based on the goals of the research or evaluation study.

   b. *Measurability* indicates concern for the sampling design to provide data appropriate for the necessary statistical computations.

   c. *Practicality* is a necessary concern for conducting sampling in any real-world situation.

   d. *Economy* refers to selecting the sample most appropriate for the study's goals with the minimum cost and effort.

2. Samples may be categorized into two kinds: subjective and objective.

   a. *Subjective* samples are selected because of the perceived importance of some attribute (e.g., most survey methods employ subjective samples).

    b. *Objective* samples are obtained by applying criteria for sample selection in an attempt to avoid the biases inherent in most subjective samples.

3. Selection of the sample is dependent upon population data.

    a. When the population data are known, then check for characteristics determined to be critical to the research or evaluation design.

    b. When the population data are unknown, report the situation as a limitation and attempt to increase the size of the sample selection to offset the possibility of sample nonrepresentativeness.

4. Determining *sample size* is critical to representativeness.

    a. As the sample size increases, the chances improve for obtaining scores from the extremes of the distribution and the standard deviation will more closely approximate that of the total population.

    b. Large samples are required when: total population is divided into subsets; population is comprised of a wide range of variables; a large number of uncontrolled variables are interacting and it is desirable to minimize their separate effects.

    c. Sample size is a consideration in some correlational techniques (e.g., absolute minimum sample of 10 for Spearman rank order; Chi square requires expected frequencies of greater than 5 in more than 80 percent of the cells).

    d. Generally, the statistical dividing line between large and small samples is a sample of 30.

    e. Data are normally considered fragile when the data producing sample falls below 60 percent to 70 percent of the selected sample.

5. The *standard error of the mean* indicates how far an obtained mean score can deviate from the population mean, thus giving an approximation of a sample's representativeness.

    a. Two items are needed to actually compute the standard error of the mean: the size of the sample and the population parameter.

    b. The standard error of the mean is directly proportional to the standard deviation of the population and inversely proportional to the size of the sample.

B. KINDS OF SAMPLES.

1. *Purposive sampling* is arbitrarily selecting a sample because there is some evidence that it is representative of the total population. No statistical analysis is intended (e.g., a certain region of the country

has consistently voted for the winning presidential candidate and a pollster selects his sample from only this region).

2. *Incidental* (also called *Haphazard* or *Available*) *sampling* is choosing a sample simply because items or subjects are available. External validity, or generalizability, is extremely weak (e.g., a psychology professor chooses his students for the sample simply because they are a "captive audience" to answer his questionnaire).

3. *Quota sampling* is based upon dividing the population into subgroups and drawing a sample to fulfill a specific quota. Units usually represent some significant characteristic of the total population (e.g., a researcher asks his questions of the first fifty people who pass by him on the assumption that they are representative of the total population).

4. *Judgment sampling* is drawing a sample based upon an expert choice or "best guess" representativeness (e.g., a researcher chooses ten schools within a very large school system as representative of all schools within the system).

5. *Random sampling* is making a selection in such a way that every item or subject in the total population has an equal chance of being chosen for the sample.

   a. Random sampling is generally accepted as sufficient evidence that the basic underlying assumptions of the parametric statistical procedures have been met.

   b. Techniques for randomization usually include applying a table of random digits to the entire population, or "fishbowl" technique (e.g., a General draws selective service numbers from a bowl to determine future draftees).

6. *Stratified Random sampling* insures that each category, when the data are so classified, is proportionately represented in the sample (e.g., a school has 1,000 students—700 males and 300 females—from which a sample of ten students is required for the study; therefore, seven males are selected from the stratum of males and three females from the stratum of females).

7. *Systematic sampling* determines a rationale for routinized selection. True chance is eliminated because all successive selections are predetermined by the very first selection (e.g., a researcher selects every tenth name listed from an alphabetized roster of the entire population).

8. *Cluster sampling* subdivides the population in clusters or large blocks and then randomly selects items or subjects. Usually used as a practical approach in very large population studies where preparation, cost,

and administration of other techniques would be prohibitive (e.g., a researcher wishes to randomly select teachers from throughout a large state; but, because of prohibitive factors, cannot truly randomize, and therefore, randomly selects school districts within the state, utilizing the teachers from the chosen districts as the sample).

C. *MATRIX SAMPLING* is an alternative to many kinds of traditional sampling in testing where all examinees complete all test items. In matrix sampling, only some of the examinees complete some of the items. This method provides data on how groups perform but *not* how individuals perform.

  Example: A state wishes to learn the reading and mathematics performance of the pupils within its boundaries, but the goals of the reading and mathematics programs throughout the state are too diverse and the numbers of pupils too large to permit any practical administration of testing all students on all test items; thus, matrix sampling is implemented.

  1. In matrix sampling, procedures and examinee sample are randomly identified and an item sample is also randomly identified; a matrix to match students to items is constructed.

  2. Advantages of matrix sampling include: reduced test time per student; suitable for testing a large domain of items; may be less threatening to examinees.

  3. Disadvantages of matrix sampling include: no comparison of examinees is possible; examinees have no personal "stake" and performance may not be at optimal level; deceptively difficult to construct item domains; difficult to coordinate logistics.

DETERMINING SAMPLE SIZE FOR RESEARCH ACTIVITIES[1]

The table below indicates the number required for a sample from a given population. This table assumes significance at the .05 level of confidence.

The following formula has been devised and may be used to determine sample size for population sizes not listed in the table or for determining sample size at different confidence levels.

$s = X^2 NP(1 - P) \div d^2(N - 1) + X^2 P(1 - P).$

s = required sample size.

X^2 = the table value of chi-square for 1 degree of freedom at the desired confidence level (3.841).

N = the population size.

P = the population proportion (assumed to be .50 since this would provide the maximum sample size).

d = the degree of accuracy expressed as a proportion (.05).

N	S	N	S	N	S
10	10	220	140	1200	291
15	14	230	144	1300	297
20	19	240	148	1400	302
25	24	250	152	1500	306
30	28	260	155	1600	310
35	32	270	159	1700	313
40	36	280	162	1800	317
45	40	290	165	1900	320
50	44	300	169	2000	322
55	48	320	175	2200	327
60	52	340	181	2400	331
65	56	360	186	2600	335
70	59	380	191	2800	338
75	63	400	196	3000	341
80	66	420	201	3500	346
85	70	440	205	4000	351
90	73	460	210	4500	354
95	76	480	214	5000	357
100	80	500	217	6000	361
110	86	550	226	7000	364
120	92	600	234	8000	367
130	97	650	242	9000	368
140	103	700	248	10000	370
150	108	750	254	15000	375
160	113	800	260	20000	377
170	118	850	265	30000	379
180	123	900	269	40000	380
190	127	950	274	50000	381
200	132	1000	278	75000	382
210	136	1100	285	100000	384

Note: N is population size; S is sample size.

[1]From "Determining Sample Size for Research Activities," by Krejcie, R. V., and Morgan, D. W., in *Educational and Psychological Measurement,* 1970, 30, 607–610.

REFERENCES

Cochran, W. G. *Sampling Techniques.* (2nd Ed.) New York, NY: Wiley, 1963.

Guilford, J. P. and Fruchter, B. *Fundamental Statistics in Psychology and Education.* New York, NY: McGraw-Hill, 1973.

Kish, L. *Survey Sampling.* New York, NY: Wiley, 1965.

Krejcie, R. V. and Morgan, D. W. "Determining Sample Size for Research Activities," *Educational and Psychological Measurement,* 30 (April 1970), 607-610.

Popham, J. W. (Ed.) *Evaluation in Education: Current Applications.* Berkeley, CA: McCutchon Publishing, 1974.

FACTOR ANALYSIS

Factor analysis is a statistical procedure that allows the researcher to tell numerically or quantitatively when different things apparently mean the same thing to a person. Its ability to describe relationships is an extension of the correlation coefficient. Thus, when presented an array of correlation coefficients for a set of variables, factor-analytic techniques enable the user to see whether some *underlying* pattern of relationships exists such that the data may be "rearranged" or "reduced" to a smaller set of factors or components. In this fashion, the single most distinctive characteristic of factor analysis is its data-reduction capability.

A. USES OF FACTOR ANALYSIS

1. Exploratory: the exploration and detection of patterning of variables with a view to the discovery of new concepts and a possible reduction of data.
2. Confirmatory: the testing of hypotheses about the structuring of variables in terms of the expected number of significant factors and factor loadings.
3. Measuring devices: the construction of indices to be used as new variables in later analyses.

B. STEPS AND TYPES OF FACTOR ANALYSIS

Steps in Factor Analysis	Major Options	Key References to the Literature
1. Preparation of correlation matrix	a. Correlation between variables	a. R-type factoring
	b. Correlation between units	b. Q-type factoring
2. Extraction of initial factors	a. Defined factors	a. Principal component solution
	b. Inferred factors	b. Classical or common component solution
3. Rotation to terminal factors	a. Uncorrelated factors	a. Orthogonal factors or rotation

C. FACTOR ANALYSIS PROCEDURES

1. Preparation of the correlation matrix; e.g., the user has data on ten individuals in terms of eight social characteristics.

   a. He could calculate the correlation between each pair of social characteristics (R-factor analysis).

   b. He could calculate the correlation between each pair of individuals (Q-factor analysis).

2. Extraction of initial factors.

   a. The first principal component is viewed as the single best summary of linear relationships exhibited in the data; the second as the second best, etc., provided the one is orthogonal to the other.

   b. The second component is the linear combination of variables that accounts for the most residual variance after the effect of the first component is removed from the data.

   c. Subsequent components are defined similarly until all the variance in the data is exhausted.

   d. Usually the first few components explain most of the variance in the data and are retained for further rotation.

3. Rotation to terminal factors.

   a. There are many statistically equivalent ways to define the underlying dimensions of the same set of data.

   b. Initial solutions extract orthogonal factors in the order of their importance.

   c. *Orthogonal* factors are uncorrelated or independent, while *oblique* factors may be correlated.

   d. The first factor extracted orthogonally tends to be a general factor and, as such, tends to load significantly on every variable.

   e. The second and following factors tend to be bipolar; i.e., approximately half of the variables have positive loadings, the other half, negative.

Comparison Between Two Factor Loadings

	Unrotated factors		Rotated factors	
VARA	.75	.63	.14	.95
VARB	.69	.57	.14	.90
VARC	.80	.49	.18	.92
VARD	.85	-.42	.94	.09
VARE	.76	-.42	.92	.07

Example 1:

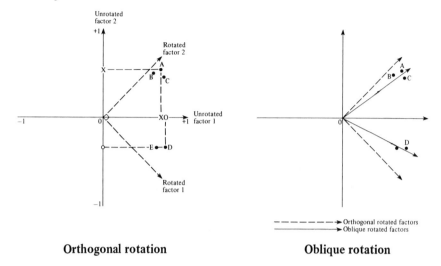

Orthogonal rotation   **Oblique rotation**

Observations on the above Example 1:

1. On the *unrotated first factor,* all variables load very high.

2. On the *unrotated second factor,* Variables A, B, C are moderately high in a positive direction, while Variables D, E are moderately high in a negative direction.

3. From inspection of the figure and table, it is obvious that there are two clusters of variables: A, B, C go together, as do D, E.

4. Note that Variable D loads high on *rotated factor 1* but almost zero on *rotated factor 2.*

5. On the other hand, Variable A loads very high on *rotated factor 2* but almost zero on *rotated factor 1.*

6. The clustering or patterning of these variables into two groups is more obvious after the rotation than before, even though the relative position or configuration of the variables remains unchanged.

Example 2:

L. L. Thurstone, in his classic work, *The Vectors of the Mind,* posited that in addition to a general mental ability (G), there were certain other primary mental abilities (a, b, c ... etc.) which could account for much of one's intellectual behavior.

Suppose, for illustrative purposes, Thurstone had administered nine intelligence tests and had identified *three factors* of mental abilities. If specific mental abilities correlated "perfectly" with some tests and not at all with others, these "perfect" factor loadings might be illustrated as follows:

| Tests | Mental Ability | | |
	a	b	c
1.	X	O	O
2.	X	O	O
3.	X	O	O
4.	O	X	O
5.	O	X	O
6.	O	X	O
7.	O	O	X
8.	O	O	X
9.	O	O	X

Observations on the above Example 2:

1. Simply stated, Tests 1, 2, and 3 correlate perfectly with Mental Ability *a* but not at all with mental abilities *b* or *c*.

2. Statisticians call this "perfect" or "high" or "pure" factor loading.

3. A similar logic holds true for remaining groups of tests and their respective correlations with other mental abilities.

Example 3:

A researcher wishes to develop a Semantic Differential instrument by means of which students would be able to evaluate selected "Teacher Behaviors." He starts with a rather long "laundry list" of bipolar adjectives, each chosen to describe a human element in teaching and an approximate opposite.

Factor analysis was applied to a large number of student responses who had used this list to evaluate one of their teachers. This analysis reduced the pairs of adjectives to four factors, thereby informing the researcher that people could not use each adjective pair differently from every other one in making their judgments. Basically, only four distinctions could be made, each represented by a factor.

Pictorially, the four clusterings might look something like the following:

TEACHER BEHAVIORS

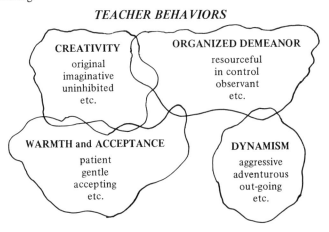

Observations on the above Example 3:

1. All pairs of adjectives may not represent perfect opposites or complete opposites.

2. Because of ambiguity in our use of words, perfect opposites would be difficult to arrive at without pairing a word with its negative form; e.g., "creative/noncreative," "original/unoriginal," etc.

3. The use of an adjective and its negative form throughout a Semantic Differential instrument should be avoided because, informationally, it is like giving only one adjective.

4. All pairs used should represent opposites in some meaningful sense.

COMPLETED INSTRUMENT

Teacher Observed   Observer   Date

Place an X in that one space of the seven between each adjective pair that best indicates your perception of the teacher's behavior. The closer you place your X toward one adjective or the other, the better you think that adjective describes the teacher.

1.	ORIGINAL	—: —: —: —: —: —: —	CONVENTIONAL
2.	PATIENT	—: —: —: —: —: —: —	IMPATIENT
3.	COLD	—: —: —: —: —: —: —	WARM
4.	HOSTILE	—: —: —: —: —: —: —	AMIABLE
5.	CREATIVE	—: —: —: —: —: —: —	ROUTINIZED
6.	INHIBITED	—: —: —: —: —: —: —	UNINHIBITED
7.	ICONOCLASTIC	—: —: —: —: —: —: —	RITUALISTIC
8.	GENTLE	—: —: —: —: —: —: —	HARSH
9.	UNFAIR	—: —: —: —: —: —: —	FAIR
10.	CAPRICIOUS	—: —: —: —: —: —: —	PURPOSEFUL
11.	CAUTIOUS	—: —: —: —: —: —: —	EXPERIMENTING
12.	DISORGANIZED	—: —: —: —: —: —: —	ORGANIZED
13.	UNFRIENDLY	—: —: —: —: —: —: —	SOCIABLE
14.	RESOURCEFUL	—: —: —: —: —: —: —	UNCERTAIN
15.	RESERVED	—: —: —: —: —: —: —	OUTSPOKEN
16.	IMAGINATIVE	—: —: —: —: —: —: —	EXACTING
17.	ERRATIC	—: —: —: —: —: —: —	SYSTEMATIC
18.	AGGRESSIVE	—: —: —: —: —: —: —	PASSIVE
19.	ACCEPTING (PEOPLE)	—: —: —: —: —: —: —	CRITICAL
20.	QUIET	—: —: —: —: —: —: —	BUBBLY
21.	OUTGOING	—: —: —: —: —: —: —	WITHDRAWN
22.	IN CONTROL	—: —: —: —: —: —: —	ON THE RUN
23.	FLIGHTY	—: —: —: —: —: —: —	CONSCIENTIOUS
24.	DOMINANT	—: —: —: —: —: —: —	SUBMISSIVE
25.	OBSERVANT	—: —: —: —: —: —: —	PREOCCUPIED
26.	INTROVERTED	—: —: —: —: —: —: —	EXTROVERTED
27.	ASSERTIVE	—: —: —: —: —: —: —	SOFT-SPOKEN
28.	TIMID	—: —: —: —: —: —: —	ADVENTUROUS

1st Factor – Creativity: Items 1, 5, 6, 7, 11, 16, 28

2nd Factor – Dynamism (Dominance and Energy): Items 15, 18, 20, 21, 24, 26, 27

3rd Factor — Organized Demeanor (Organization and Control): Items 10, 12, 14, 17, 22, 23, 25

4th Factor — Warmth and Acceptance: Items 2, 3, 4, 8, 9, 13, 19

5. The naming of factors is left to the researcher; but it should have an overall relationship to the items in the cluster (e.g., the factor labeled *dynamism* seemed to be a combination of *dominance* and *energy*.

6. The finished instrument contains twenty-eight pairs of bipolar adjectives; for reliability purposes, seven pairs were used (rather than one, or two, or five) to measure each factor.

7. The seven pairs with the highest factor loadings were used in each case.

REFERENCES

Harman, H. H. *Modern Factor Analysis.* (2nd Ed.) Chicago, IL: University of Chicago Press, 1963.

Mulaik, S. A. *The Foundations of Factor Analysis.* New York, NY: McGraw-Hill, 1972.

UNIT IV

QUALITY CONTROL

	Page
RESEARCH DESIGNS.	83
SOURCES OF ERRORS.	91
RELIABILITY AND VALIDITY	97
ITEM ANALYSIS	101
TEST ITEM BIAS	105
FORMULATING HYPOTHESES	109

RESEARCH DESIGNS

Research designs are simply methods of organizing the search for answers to questions about experimental treatments. They provide a structure about which an educational program may be tested to determine its effectiveness, as well as offering some insights into how the same program may operate in other situations. The designs differ in the degree to which they provide information about a program and the degree to which generalizations about the potential for success of the same program in different settings can be made. The purposes of the particular study will dictate whether or not it is important to generalize the findings; and, the circumstances may limit the freedom one has in selecting any particular research design.

Research designs are judged for strength by their ability to control errors in validity (see VALIDITY). While there are any number of research designs, there is general agreement upon the categorization of designs into pre-experimental, true-experimental, and quasi-experimental groups.

A. CONTROLLING VARIANCES

1. *Maximize the experimental variance;* or, "pull apart" experimental conditions by choosing as dissimilar conditions as possible (e.g., in evaluating types of reading instructional methods, select for study methods which are not similar).

2. *Control the extraneous variables* means to nullify or isolate those variables not necessary to the purposes of the study and which may influence the variable under investigation.

   a. Eliminate the variable as a variable (e.g., if intelligence can influence the variable under study, say, attitudes toward mathematics, choose subjects of only one intelligence range).

   b. Randomization is the best method for controlling the extraneous variables.

    c. Build the extraneous variable into the design as an independent variable (e.g., if one is worried that the variance of sex—males versus females—may influence the study, add sex as an independent variable and compare sex difference on the dependent variable.)

    d. *Matching subjects* is a corollary to building the variable into the design; generally, this is the least preferred method.

    e. Statistical control has the ability to isolate variables.

3. *Minimize the error variance* is to reduce the possibility of random fluctuations and statistical errors of measurement; the total effect of error variance is unpredictable.

B. PRE-EXPERIMENTAL RESEARCH DESIGNS

1. In the *One-shot case study* design, a single instance is carefully studied and compared with other events only casually observed or remembered.

    a. Advantage is the utility and practicality for real-world exploration into educational programs.

    b. Disadvantage is the very weak (almost nonexistent) ability to control for errors of validity.

2. The *One-group pretest posttest* design merely tests a single group before and after some treatment.

    a. Advantage is the comparison between performances by the same subjects.

    b. Disadvantage is the inability to accurately assess whether or not the differences are due to the treatment or confounding extraneous variables.

3. The *Static-group* comparison applies a treatment to one group of subjects and then posttests two groups, the one group that received the treatment and another group that did not receive treatment, for comparisons.

    a. Advantage is this design can provide group comparisons to evaluate a program after it is completed.

    b. Disadvantage is the equivalence of the groups is unknown.

C. TRUE-EXPERIMENTAL RESEARCH DESIGNS

1. In the *Pretest-posttest control group* design, two randomized groups are tested before the treatment to determine prior knowledge. Only one group is given the treatment and then posttest measures are taken on both groups to determine respective changes.

a. Probably the most used of the true-experimental designs.

b. Minimizes control over threats to internal validity.

c. Design can be expanded to include more than one kind of treatment (e.g., testing two, three, or more kinds of reading instruction programs against only one control group in a single study.

d. Allows judgments about the treatment effectiveness either comparatively between groups or absolutely between each group and a predetermined criterion.

e. Statistical power is increased by using the pretest measure as a covariate to statistically equate the groups.

f. Disadvantage is the lack of ability to control threats to external validity (generalizing the findings to other settings).

g. Testing—particularly in attitude assessment—can become confounded with some extraneous variable (e.g., testing attitudes toward a particular political party immediately after having attended a political rally).

h. The effects of interference when several treatments are used is unknown and must be considered a liability.

2. The *Solomon four-group* design adds two groups to the standard pretest-posttest control group design. Of the two new groups, one receives the treatment and one does not; neither group is pretested and both are posttested.

a. Helps to control the threats to external validity inherent in the standard design (e.g., controls for possibility of pretest sensitizing groups to the treatment).

b. Allow to assess more accurately the effects of the pretest alone, the treatment alone, and the interaction of pretesting and treatment.

c. By disregarding pretests, analysis of variance procedures are possible.

d. Alternatively, by using pretest as a covariate, analysis of covariance procedures are possible.

e. Disadvantage is difficulty in arranging the logistics of the design.

3. *Posttest-only control group* design utilizes the last two groups of the Solomon four-group design: one group receives treatment and both groups are posttested only. Design assumes groups are equal due to random assignment.

a. Comparatively easy design to implement.

b. Used in instances when a pretest is too costly or inappropriate

Figure 1

EVALUATIVE RESEARCH DESIGNS[1],[2]

Pre-Experimental Designs

#1. One-shot Case Study
X O

#2. One-Group Pretest-Posttest Design
O X O

#3. Static-Group Comparison
X O
― ― ―
O

Quasi-Experimental Designs

#7. Time Series
O O O O X O O O O

#8. Equivalent Time Samples Design
$X_1 O X_o O X_1 O X_o O$, etc.

#9. Nonequivalent Control Group Design
O X O
― ― ―
O O

True Experimental Designs

#4. Pretest-Posttest Control Group Design
R O X O
R O   O

#5. Solomon Four-Group Design
R O X O
R O   O
R   X O
R   O

#6. Posttest-Only Control Group Design
R   X O
R   O

[1] R stands for *randomization*, X for *treatment, and* O for *observation*. A time factor is assumed when symbols are read from left to right. The broken line in designs 3 and 9 signifies that random assignment to groups has not been employed.

[2] From *Experimental and Quasi-Experimental Designs for Research*, by Donald T. Campbell and Julian C. Stanley. Chicago: Rand McNally, 1966.

A FLOWCHART FOR SELECTING
RESEARCH AND EVALUATION DESIGNS[1],[2]

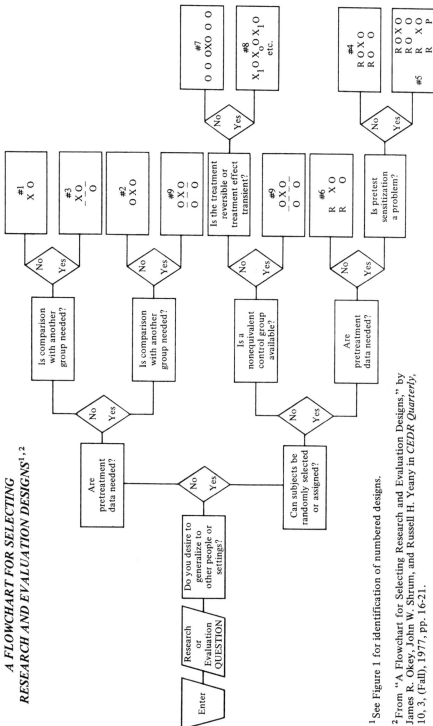

[1] See Figure 1 for identification of numbered designs.

[2] From "A Flowchart for Selecting Research and Evaluation Designs," by James R. Okey, John W. Shrum, and Russell H. Yeany in *CEDR Quarterly*, 10, 3, (Fall), 1977, pp. 16-21.

(e.g., evaluating a foreign language instructional program where students arrive with no prior knowledge of the language).

c. By eliminating any possible interaction effect of a pretest with the treatment, this design covers a weakness of design which does require a pretest.

d. Often the optimal design for applying the statistical t-test.

e. Design requires great care in selection of a posttest instrument which is truly sensitive to changes caused by the treatment.

f. Design will not allow as powerful statistical tests as is permitted by the standard pretest-posttest control group design.

D. QUASI-EXPERIMENTAL DESIGNS

1. The *Time-series* research design is characterized by periodic measurements on the same group and with a one-time intervening treatment.

   a. Seldom achieves much acceptability in psychological research, but popularly used in physical sciences and biological research.

   b. Disadvantage is the inability to control for effects of *history* (e.g., events occurring between two measurements) upon subjects, and this design typically extends over long periods of time.

   c. If the time series is interrupted, a potential for limitations in the interaction of the treatments with the sample exists.

   d. In the absence of a control group, the experiment might be repeated in many different places by different researchers to gain external validity.

2. The *Equivalent-time samples* design is an extension of the time series design by alternating treatment and no treatment prior to each measurement.

   a. Useful design when the effects of the treatment is anticipated to be short term (e.g., studies of learning).

   b. A random sampling of time periods for each measurement is necessary (e.g., several experiments involving a single experimental group with a randomized equal sample of days between each measurement).

   c. Controls for *history*, overcoming a weakness of other time series designs.

   d. Disadvantage is the inability to generalize the findings to other subjects in other settings.

3. The *Nonequivalent-control group* design has the same structure as the standard pretest-posttest control group design with one important

exception: there is no random assignment of subjects to groups. Design assumes random assignment of treatments to groups.

a. Very popularly used in real-world school settings.

b. Often groups are prearranged natural units (e.g., classrooms, schools, etc.).

c. Regardless of design limitations, it is still superior to the one group pretest-posttest design.

d. Common problem is differing rates of maturation between the experimental and control groups.

e. "Matching" groups on some relevant criterion can add greater precision to the design.

f. Statistically equating groups through analysis of covariance procedures is possible but may involve some disputable assumptions.

g. Comparison of simple gain scores is possible utilizing t-test or analysis of variance procedures.

REFERENCES

Campbell, D. T. and Stanley, J. C. *Experimental and Quasi-Experimental Designs for Research.* Chicago, IL: Rand McNally, 1963.

Fisher, R. *The Design of Experiments* (6th Ed.) New York, NY: Hafner, 1951.

Fox, D. J. *The Research Process in Education.* New York, NY: Holt, 1969.

Isaac, S. and Michael, W. B. *Handbook in Research and Evaluation.* San Diego, CA: Robert R. Knapp, 1971.

Kerlinger, F. N. *Foundations of Behavioral Research.* (2nd Ed.) New York, NY: Holt, 1973.

Kirk, R. E. *Experimental Design Procedures for the Behavioral Sciences,* Belmont, CA: Brooks/Cole, 1968.

Okey, J. R., Shrum, J. W., and Yeany, R. H. "A Flowchart for Selecting Research and Evaluation Designs," *CEDR Quarterly,* 10, (Fall 1973) 3.

Suchman, E. A. *Evaluative Research: Principles and Practice in Public Service and Social Action Programs.* New York, NY: Russell Sage Foundation, 1967.

SOURCES OF ERRORS

Evaluation studies may be subject to errors, or infected, in two ways: through threats to validity because of faulty design and through erroneous interpretation resulting from basic infections. An awareness of these may serve to alert the evaluator to their presence and their damaging effects.

Although unobtrusive measures are often used to eliminate many reactive effects, it is virtually impossible to identify and remove all sources of error from research and evaluation studies. However, recognizing potential areas in which errors may occur and initiating the appropriate controls will help to reduce errors and lead toward more accurate findings and conclusions.

A. FACTORS JEOPARDIZING VALIDITY

1. *History* is the occurrence of events between the pretest and posttest which may be confused with the effects of the independent variable.

   a. For example, of two groups, experimental and comparison, the teachers of one group are promoted and there must be a teacher change for that group, but not the other.

2. *Maturation* is the process of change within the subjects.

   a. For example, subjects become bored, tired, etc.

3. *Testing* is the effects of testing upon the program or subsequent measurement.

   a. For example, in a short interval experimental program, the pretest has the effect of being a practice test for the posttest.

4. *Instrumentation* is something inherent in the measurement process that may result in inaccurate assessment.

   a. For example, a teacher-made test, whose reliability has not been established, is used to assess program effects.

5. *Statistical regression* is the tendency of subjects to score closer to the mean on retesting.

a. For example, subjects are selected for a program on the basis of extremely low or high scores on a test; then the program may be erroneously judged a success for lower achieving students (because they tended to score higher on the posttest) and a failure for higher achieving students (because they tended to score lower on the posttest).

6. *Selection bias* occurs when subjects participate in an experiment because of some external motivation.

   a. For example, a reading program is tested using only volunteer subjects.

7. *Experimental mortality* is the loss of subjects at different rates from comparison groups.

   a. For example, a long-term study of a health education program retains only those subjects who are willing to give up "junk foods" for a year.

8. *Selection-maturation interaction* occurs when the affects of multiple group participation is confounded with the experimental variable.

   a. For example, in a study of two psychotherapy programs, subjects are matched with "normal" persons from the population at large.

9. *Reactive or interaction effect of testing* occurs when a pretest may sensitize a subject's responsiveness to the experimental variable.

   a. For example, in a teacher in-service program, a preassessment of teachers' attitudes sensitizes them to the in-service program.

10. The *interaction effects of selection biases* and the *experimental variable* occur when these effects are confounded.

    a. For example, an experiment overcomes the weakness of interaction by using a separate sample for the pretest and the posttest.

11. *Reactive effects of experimental arrangements* occurs when an experimental setting is unique to the variable under study and precludes generalizations to nonexperimental settings.

    a. For example, a teacher variable study utilizes teachers with unusually divergent and dynamic personalities in a special setting and the results are erroneously generalized to other teacher groups.

12. *Multiple-treatment interference* occurs when the same subjects (especially one-group designs) are used in experiments of multiple treatments.

    a. For example, a study of various foreign languages and instructional techniques involving only one group is erroneously judged by neglecting to account for the fact that learning each succeeding language is usually easier than its predecessor.

B. REACTIVE CONCERNS

1. *Hawthorne effect* occurs when the behavior of subjects changes because they are aware of their special status.

    a. For example, in a study of light conditions on work performance, subjects perform better than before the experiment regardless of the level of light because they know they are being included in a special test.

2. *Halo effect* refers to biased ratings—either high or low—to some attribute, skill, etc., on the basis of a more global impression.

    a. For example, a housewife may select a certain brand of soap because she likes the movie star who advertises it.

3. *Placebo* (or *blind*) *effect* is the notion of exposing experimental and control groups to treatments that are not so far apart as to render comparisons meaningless.

    a. For example, in an experiment on methods of mathematics instruction, both groups should be exposed to reasonable methods.

    b. *Double blind* refers to a situation in which the researcher does not know which group is the experimental and which the control.

4. *John Henry effect* occurs when the performance of a control group, placed in competition with an experimental group, will far outpace what they ordinarily would do because of feeling threatened or a "we'll show them" attitude.

    a. For example, in a study comparing the work output of a machine with human workers, the people try harder fearing a loss of their jobs if the experimental machine outperforms them.

5. *Expectancy* (or Pygmalion) *effect* refers to a researcher directing his attention to seeing those attributes he "expects to see."

    a. For example, a teacher is told by the principal that one of her classrooms has all gifted children and another has all slow children; the teacher interprets a noisy atmosphere as "creativity" in one room and "disruption" in the other.

6. *Response sets* refers to how a test is structured may elicit certain answers.

    a. For example, a teacher may structure a multiple choice test for ease of scoring such that response "C" is correct for all items; students would tend to answer "C" to items they do not know on the basis of having answered all known items "C."

7. *"Figures prove . . . "* is the idea that numbers carry no meaning themselves; their meaning rests in their use.

   a. Disraeli said: "There are lies, damned lies, and statistics!"

   b. Huff, *How to Lie with Statistics.*

   c. For example, an advertisement reads: "80% of the doctors interviewed" can mean four of only five questioned.

8. *Law of the instrument* is the human inclination to become attached to a particular instrument and apply it to every problem.

   a. For example, the old saying, "Give a small boy a hammer and he will find that everything in the environment needs pounding!"

9. *Elementalism* is the notion that one thing causes everything.

   a. For example, a counselor erroneously believes that a suicide is caused solely by the reason stated in the suicide note.

10. *Post hoc, ergo propter hoc:* "After this, therefore because of this."

   a. For example, superstitious belief that the sun rises because of a rooster crowing just prior to its appearance every day.

11. *Ad verecundiam:* "According to the truth . . . "

   a. For example, buying a poor product simply because it is endorsed by a known authority.

   b. G. B. Shaw said: "How can I tell if I like a play if I don't know its author?"

12. *Secundum quid:* "According to which . . . "

   a. The fallacy of inadequate sampling.

   b. For example, superstition of bad luck following walking under a ladder and forgetting the tremendous number of times one has walked under a ladder with no ill consequences.

13. *Ad hominem:* "To the man rather than the issue."

   a. The fallacy of personality clouds the issue.

   b. Evaluation report should cover all findings, not just selected findings which support desired outcomes.

   c. For example, disliking a speech because the orator has not gone past the seventh grade.

14. *Tu quogue:* "You also . . . (you're another! So's your old man.)."

   a. Two wrongs do not make a right.

   b. For example, stopped for speeding and complaining that others are driving faster than you were: "Why stop me—look at them!"

REFERENCES

Anderson, S. B., Ball, S., and Murphy, R. T. *Encyclopedia of Educational Evaluation.* San Francisco, CA: Jossey-Bass, 1975.

Argyris, C. "Some Unintended Consequences of Rigorous Research." *Psychological Bulletin,* 70 (September 1968), pp. 185-197.

Campbell, D. T., and Stanley, J. C. *Experimental and Quasi-Experimental Designs for Research.* Chicago, IL: Rand-McNally, 1966.

Gephart, W. J. and Antonoplos, D. P. "The Effects of Expectancy and Other Research-Biasing Factors." *Phi Delta Kappan,* 50 (June 1969), pp. 579-583.

Rosenthal, R. and Jacobson, L. *Pygmalion in the Classroom.* New York, NY: Holt, 1968.

Suchman, E. A. *Evaluative Research: Principles and Practice in Public Service and Social Action Programs.* New York, NY: Russell Sage Foundation, 1967.

Trow, M. "Methodological Problems in the Evaluation of Innovation." In M. C. Wittrock and D. E. Wiley (eds.), *The Evaluation of Instruction: Issues and Problems.* New York, NY: Holt, 1970, pp. 289-305.

RELIABILITY AND VALIDITY

Despite much experience and many sophisticated measurement techniques, the responsible researcher recognizes that error exists in the assessment of any psychological trait. Reliability and validity are estimates of the measurement error inherent in all psychological data. A "perfectly reliable" and "perfectly valid" measurement is one that is completely free of all sources of error.

Reliability and validity are very important in both theoretical investigations and practical work. While there is nothing inherently magic about these terms, in measurement they are like money: the lack of it is a real problem. Of these two properties, validity is the more important; however, reliability is a necessary, if not wholly complete, condition for validity. The theory grounding these two concepts is complex; further, the issue is complicated by the fact that the characteristic being measured (e.g., aptitude, skill, etc.) may itself be unstable and fluctuate regardless of the measurement.

A. **RELIABILITY** is the degree of stability and consistency which a scale yields when a trait is measured a number of times. The index of reliability coefficient.

   Example: If a teacher measures the reading achievement of her class and ranks pupils highest to lowest, and one week later retests the pupils, the degree to which she could expect them to retain their relative standing is a measure of the test's reliability.

   1. Different methods of determining reliability coefficients account for different sources of error.

      a. *Correlation coefficients* indicate how two sets of scores are related.

      b. *Internal consistency* methods reveal the homogeneity of the items in a test.

2. Three popular methods of establishing correlation coefficients are: test-retest method; alternate-forms method; split-half method.

3. The test-retest method correlates scores on the same test given at different times.

   a. Advantages: Close to the conceptual notion of reliability; requires only a single scale; holds constant the items used, thus eliminating the unreliability due to differences between items.

   b. Disadvantages: The fact that the subject has been tested on one occasion may influence his score on subsequent measurement; the ideal time interval between tests is unknown (most investigators use from two to six weeks).

4. The alternate-forms method indicates the correlation between two comparable forms of the same scale.

   a. Advantages: Effects of the time interval and of responding to one scale upon the response to the other is minimized.

   b. Disadvantages: Two forms are necessary.

5. The split-half method is a correlation between comparable parts of the same scale.

   a. To estimate the reliability of the total scale, the Spearman-Brown prophecy formula is applied to the correlation coefficient obtained for the two "equivalent" halves.

   b. Advantages: Same as alternate-forms method and requires only one scale.

   c. Disadvantages: Does not estimate time interval reliability.

6. Internal consistency reliability is based on item statistics.

   a. Coefficients based upon total numbers of items, the standard deviation and either item variance (Kuder-Richardson Formula 20) or the test mean (Kuder-Richardson Formula 21).

   b. Coefficients for item homogeneity can also use Cronbach's "alpha' index.

B. **VALIDITY** is, simply, the degree to which a scale measures what it is supposed to measure. However, the concept of validity is complex. The various types of validity indicate how well a test is capable of achieving certain aims.

   Example: If an employment interviewer administers a test to determine the motivation to achieve of a prospective employee, the degree to which the interviewer may speculate about the applicant's "true" achievement motivations (assuming they remain constant) is an estimate of the test's *construct validity*.

1. While there are numerous types of validity, some theoreticians claim that *construct validity* is the most important and all other types are subsets of it.

2. *Construct validity* is the "degree to which scores on a measure permit inferences about underlying traits" (Anderson, 1975, p. 459).

   a. According to APA *Standards for Educational and Psychologial Tests,* 'Evidence of construct validity is not found in a single study; rather, judgments . . . are based upon an accumulation of research results" (1974, p. 30).

   b. It is estimated from the relationship between the measure in question to other measures.

   c. Methods of estimating: Known-groups technique (e.g., two groups holding differing attitudes toward a given object); involve correlation matrices (multi-trait, multi-method matrix technique).

3. *Content validity* refers to how well a measure captures the objectives of a program.

   a. Usually is subjective and judgmental.

   b. Not to be confused with *Face Validity* (the superficial appearance of items).

4. *Criterion-related validity* indicates how highly scores correlate to an external criterion.

   a. Varies widely from situation to situation.

   b. Establishing the criterion can be complex and easily misleading.

   c. Sometimes takes the form of expectancy tables.

REFERENCES

American Psychological Association. *Standards for Educational and Psychological Tests.* Washington, D.C., 1974.

Anderson, S. B. and others. *Encyclopedia of Educational Evaluation.* San Francisco, CA: Jossey-Bass, 1975.

Campbell, D. T. and Stanley, J. C. *Experimental and Quasi-Experimental Designs for Research.* Chicago, IL: Rand McNally, 1966.

Cronbach, L. J. *Essentials of Psychological Testing* (3rd Ed.). New York, NY: Harper, 1970.

Mehrens, W. and Ebel, R. (Eds.). *Principles of Educational and Psychological Measurement.* Skokie, IL: Rand McNally, 1967.

Thorndike, Robert L. *Educational Measurement* (2nd Ed.). Washington, D.C.: American Council on Education, 1971.

ITEM ANALYSIS

Magnusson (1966) suggests that a total test can have no properties which are not derived from the individual items or their relationship; therefore, an analysis of the individual items of a test as they relate to each other and to the test as a whole is important to any test. Item analysis is the process through which a testmaker measures a testing instrument in its discrete parts and determines individual item effectiveness/ineffectiveness for revision and measurement purposes.

Hence, item analysis is defined as a procedure to increase the reliability and validity of a test by separately evaluating each test item to determine whether or not that item discriminates in the same way the overall test is intended to discriminate (Isaac & Michael, 1971).

A. PURPOSES OF ITEM ANALYSIS

1. *Item difficulty:* the percent of high/low students who answer a test item correctly (p-value).

   a. A single test item is regarded as being difficult/easy through an examination of its p-value—the farther from a .50 value, the greater the difficulty/ease of that item.

   b. The difficulty index of an item is never considered alone, but always in relation to other indices computed.

2. *Item discrimination:* the precision in which a given trait, measured by a given item, indicates differences in group (high/low) responses.

   a. The division point for dividing a response group into high/low sections is arbitrary, but common practice is to split the data into halves—upper and lower.

   b. To increase the contrast, compare the upper third with the lowest third, or the upper quarter with the lowest quarter.

c. A single test item is regarded as having perfect positive discriminating power if everyone in the overall high-scoring group and no one in the overall low-scoring groups answers it correctly.

d. When a larger proportion of the low-scoring group answers an item correctly than does a proportion of the high-scoring group, the item is said to have a negative discrimination value.

3. *Item internal consistency:* measurement of the degree to which test-takers make comparable scores on different parts of a test taken at a single sitting.

4. *Item reliability:* the consistency/accuracy of an item to make possible the obtaining of similar results upon reiteration; i.e., the degree to which measurement of an item is free from random influence.

5. *Item validity:* the extent to which a test item measures what it is supposed to measure.

a. The ability of an item to distinguish between those knowing and those not knowing particular material related to the test item (English & English, 1958).

B. RELIABILITY AND RELIABILITY COEFFICIENTS

1. A test is reliable to the extent that it can report virtually the same scores in retestings.

a. Practically, it is the correlation between two testings of the same group of individuals.

2. *Coefficient of Stability* (Test-Retest)

a. Test-retest involves giving the same test on two separate occasions approximately a week apart.

b. Some advocate a greater time difference than a week—ten days to two weeks.

c. Too short a difference in time between testings subjects the responses to recall effect; too long a time between testings endangers responses through history and maturation of subjects.

d. Correlation between testings is established using the Phi Coefficient.

e. The test-retest method of establishing reliability is generally the most suitable for criterion-referenced tests.

3. *Coefficient of Equivalence* (Alternate, Parallel, or Equivalent Forms).

a. Two equivalent forms of a test are administered to the same group of individuals and the pairs of scores are correlated.

b. Since this involves two different representative samples of items, this is, in terms of test theory, the most desirable index of test reliability.

c. If the correlation is to be meaningful, test content, types of items, instructions, test statistics (minimum level of performance, deviation scores), etc., must be approximately the same.

4. *Coefficient of Internal Consistency* (Split-half).

a. Where only a single administration of a test is practical for correlation purposes, the test is divided into two halves.

b. A common procedure is to use odd and even items.

c. It does not matter that some items measure different specifics; the gross test scores of the two halves measure the same thing.

d. The Spearman-Brown formula is usually applied to the result.

e. This method should *not* be used with timed tests.

f. This method is suitable only for criterion-referenced tests that are fairly homogenous.

5. *Method of Rational Equivalence* (Isaac & Michael, 1971).

a. The Kuder-Richardson formulas 20 and 21 provide relatively conservative estimates of the Coefficient of Equivalence.

b. Greater reliance can be placed on this method if the test is highly homogenous and the assumption of equal or near-equal item difficulty is met.

C. IMPROVING THE RELIABILITY OF A TEST

1. Test reliability is improved by editing poor test items and by lengthening the test.

2. The Spearman-Brown Formula permits us to estimate what reliability the test would have if it were lengthened or shortened.

a. This formula assumes that in the lengthening or shortening of the test, the nature of the test is not changed.

b. Extreme increases in length may be counter-productive by introducing a fatigue and/or boredom factor.

3. Lengthening a test increases its reliability significantly, but has a much smaller effect on validity.

The following formula will tell you how many times to lengthen a test to obtain any desired reliability:

$$\frac{\text{(The reliability you want) X (1−the reliability you got)}}{\text{(The reliability you got) X (1−the reliability you want)}}$$

If you want .90 and got .60, this becomes:

$$\frac{.90 \text{ X } (1-.60)}{.60 \text{ X } (1-.90)} = 6 \text{ times longer test needed}$$

REFERENCES

Davis, F. B. *Item Analysis Data.* Cambridge, MA: Harvard University, 1946.

English, H. B. and English, A. C. *A Comprehensive Dictionary of Psychological and Psychoanalytical Terms.* New York, NY: David McKay Company, 1958.

Isaac, S. and Michael, W B. *Handbook in Research and Evaluation.* San Diego, CA: Robert R. Knapp, 1971.

Magnusson, D. *Test Theory.* Reading, MA: Addison-Wesley Publishing Company, 1966.

Wilson, J. A., Robeck, M. C. and Michael, W. B. *Psychological Foundations of Learning and Teaching.* New York, NY: McGraw-Hill Book Company, 1974.

TEST ITEM BIAS

The question of test bias in any testing environment strikes at the heart of test validity (see Reliability and Validity). Public controversy over tests and their use has raged ever since the mass testing movement began during World War I. Evaluators need to be aware of the terms and issues involved in test bias, as well as be familiar with the specifics of detecting and correcting biased items in some tests.

Test bias extends beyond the testing instrument itself and includes the way in which test scores are used.

A. DEFINITION

1. *Bias* is the systematic under- or overestimation of a population parameter by a statistic based upon samples drawn from the population.

2. A test item is biased if individuals of equal ability have different probabilities of attaining the item correct.

3. *Discrimination* in test methodology is to show a reliable (i.e., statistically significant) difference between individuals on some item or test statistic.

B. CONCEPTS OF FAIRNESS/UNFAIRNESS

1. Bias, when used by evaluators, is a statistical term and is to be kept distinct from the concept of fairness or unfairness.

2. The unfair or discriminatory *use* of test results does not in itself constitute test bias.

C. IMPROPER CONCEPTS OF BIAS

1. *Egalitarian fallacy* is the notion that all human populations are essentially identical or equal in the trait being measured, and, therefore,

any difference between populations in the distribution of test scores is evidence of test bias.

2. *Culture-bound fallacy* is a criticism of the test's content validity based upon conjecture. An opinion is expressed that some terms used in test items (e.g., *Sonata* or *"Hamlet's"* author) are culture bound and some groups have not experienced cultural backgrounds that include these kinds of knowledge. The argument assumes that casual inspection or subjective judgement can identify culturally skewed items.

3. *Standardization fallacy* presumes that because a test was standardized on a specific given population it is *ipso facto* biased when used in any other population. The use of a test with each and every population must be independently examined. Reliability and validity must be investigated for each group. Simply renorming a test for use with a population other than the standardization group does not accomplish anything of fundamental significance.

D. PROCEDURES TO DETECT BIAS

(Abbreviations used on following chart)

1. Analysis of Variance (ANOVA) — using item scores the differences between many means are compared simultaneously. Central to the approach is the interaction between groups and items.

2. Transformed Item Difficulties (TID) — total scores as well as individual item scores are used; percent correct (p-values) are transformed to a standard score (z-scores) for each group included.

3. Point Biserial Correlation (PBIS) — total scores are correlated to the response of each examinee; correlation magnitudes are computed for two groups at a time.

4. Chi Square (CHI) — a goodness-of-fit test in which equal proportions of each group considered are expected to achieve similarly on items; a comparison is made to actual performance of groups.

5. Factor Analysis (FACTOR) — correlations are computed for correct and incorrect responses to each item; similar factors are grouped into a matrix and a pattern of factor loading is devised.

6. Item characteristic Curve (ICC) — part of latent trait methodology several approaches possible but generally the ability level of individuals within each group examined is assessed against an established difficulty level for each item.

7. Response Fail Analysis (RFA) — a distractor analysis in which the distribution of responses to distractors for different groups is examined.

SUMMARY OF SELECTED ITEM BIAS DETECTION TECHNIQUES

METHOD	FOCUS OF ANALYSIS	ASPECT EXAMINED	COMPUTATION EASE	COMPUTATIONAL AIDS NECESSARY	EASE OF INTERPRETATION	MEASURE OF BIAS	SAMPLE SIZE NEEDED	ESTIMATE OF FUNCTION
ANOVA	Interaction Between Group Membership and Correct Response	Item Difficulty	Difficult	Computer Necessary	Moderate to Difficult	Significance of F for Main Effects and Interactions	Depends on the number of items; Conservative, 100 per group	Not Examined
TID	Interaction Between Group Membership and Correct Response	Item Difficulty	Simple	Hand Calculations Possible Calculator Desirable Computer Handy	Simple	Arbitrary Designation of Distance on Scatterplot	30 to 50 People per Group	Good for Difficulty Poor for Discrimination
PBIS	Difference in Item-Total Correlations Between Groups	Item-Total Correlations	Moderate to Simple	Hand Calculation Possible Calculator Desirable Computer Handy	Simple	Arbitrary Designation of Magnitude of Differences Between Correlations	50 to 100 People per Group	Poor
CHI	Difference in Proportions Attaining a Correct Response Across Total Score Categories	Item Difficulty	Moderate to Simple	Hand Calculation Possible Calculator Desirable Computer Handy	Simple	Significance of Chi-Square	100 or More per Group	Satisfactory
FACTOR	Major Loadings on Factors Which Also Have Major Group Membership Loadings	Item Intecorrelation Matrix	Difficult	Computer Necessary	Difficult	Arbitrary Designation of Magnitude of Factor Loading	Conservative Number of People 10 Times the Number of Items	Moderate
ICC	Difference in Probability of Responding Correctly	Item Difficulty, Item Discrimination, Guessing	Difficult	Computer Necessary	Difficult	Area Between ICC Curves	Conservative, 1000 per Group	Satisfactory
RFA	Difference in Proportions Selecting Distractors	Distractor Difficulty	Simple	Hand Calculation Possible Calculator Desirable Computer Handy	Simple	Significance of Chi-Square	100 or More per Group	Not Examined

From: Merz, William R. *Methods of Assessing Bias and Fairness in Tests* ARC Technical Report No. 121-79. Sacramento: Applied Research Consultants, Inc., March, 1980.

REFERENCES

Baker, F. B. "Advances in Item Analysis," *Review of Educational Research,* 47, 1977, pp. 151-178.

Fincher, C. "Differential Validity and Test Bias," *Personnel Psychology,* 28, 1975, pp. 481-500.

Ironson, G. H. and Subkoviak, M. J. "A Comparison of Several Methods of Assessing Item Bias," *Journal of Educational Measurement,* 16, 1979, pp. 209-225.

Jensen, A. R. *Bias in Mental Testing.* New York, NY: The Free Press, 1980.

Merz, W. R. *Methods of Assessing Bias and Fairness in Tests,* ARC Technical Report No. 121-79. Sacramento, CA: Applied Research Consultants, March, 1980.

Rudner, L. M., Getson, P. R., and Knight, D. L. "Biased Item Detection Techniques," *Journal of Educational Statistics,* 5 (Fall, 1980), pp. 213-233.

FORMULATING HYPOTHESES

The development of hypotheses starts with reviewing the findings of previous research in a delimited area. By exploring prior efforts, the researcher/evaluator can determine valid findings, generalizations, methods, achievements, and weaknesses of previous investigations. In addition, such a review discloses various linkages between concepts and some of the problems associated with the discerned linkages.

A. HYPOTHESIS FORMULATION

1. Hypothesis formulation is the heart of a quantitative research/evaluation report.

2. Every hypothesis indicates expected relationships among key concepts.

   a. This relationship is generally stated in terms of independence and dependence.

   b. An *independent* concept is one that influences (not necessarily causes) another concept.

   c. A *dependent* concept is one being influenced by another(s).

      Example: As education increases, church attendance increases. The independent concept is education, the dependent, church attendance.

   d. The researcher/evaluator determines which concept is independent and which is dependent on the basis of previous research and current logic.

3. A hypothesis then addresses itself to two essential questions:

   a. What are the essential concepts?

   b. What are the expected relationships between/among them?

B. RELATIONAL HYPOTHESIS

1. A relational association exists when two or more concepts covary.

   a. A relational hypothesis does not deal with causality.

   b. It relates to a relationship between two concepts that are associated strongly enough with each other to vary together.

   c. Once such interrelated concepts are identified, then researchers can focus on determining the rationale for such a relationship and on speculating on some of the probable causes of this interdependence.

   d. The treatment of causal relationships requires elaborate research designs and sophisticated statistical techniques.

2. A relational hypothesis can be stated in either directional or nondirectional terms.

   a. A *nondirectional* hypothesis suggests only that two or more concepts covary; it does not suggest the direction.

   Example: There is a relationship between X and Y.

   b. A *directional* hypothesis not only states that two or more concepts covary but also the direction in which they covary.

   Example: (Positive) The more frequently X occurs, the more frequently Y occurs

   (Negative) The more frequently X occurs, the less frequently Y occurs.

C. REPORTING HYPOTHESIS ANALYSIS THROUGH TABLES

1. Table layout should reflect the hypothesis.

   a. When a brief title is used, the dependent concept is listed first, followed by the independent concept(s).

   Example: Vote by Income and Education.

   b. A more complex title would describe succinctly the expected relationship.

2. The independent concept is placed at the top of the table, with the dependent concept at the left-hand side.

   a. Whenever the hypothesis is directional, the key cell should be in the upper left-hand corner of the table. (When nondirection, key cell position is not important.)

   Example: (Directional positive) The more frequently X occurs, the more frequently Y occurs.

VARIABLE X

		More Frequently	**Less Frequently**
VARIABLE Y	**More Frequently**	**KEY CELL**	
	Less Frequently		

Example: (Directional negative) The more frequently X occurs, the less frequently Y occurs.

VARIABLE X

		More Frequently	**Less Frequently**
VARIABLE Y	**Less Frequently**	**KEY CELL**	
	More Frequently		

3. *Findings* are reported in specifics, *conclusions* in generalities.

Example: Finding: Fifty-five percent of people who have a high income attend church often; 45 percent of the people who have a medium income attend church often; and 35 percent of the people who have a low income attend church often.

Conclusion: As people's incomes increase, they are more likely to attend church.

D. DEVELOPMENT OF THE HYPOTHESIS

Example: Research question: Is there a relationship between . . . ?

Research statement: There is a relationship between . . . .

Null hypothesis: There is no relationship between . . . .

1. Research *question* is a true research guide.
   a. The question, or set of questions, serves to identify the problem.
   b. It gives research its goal and its thrust.

2. Research *statement* is a step beyond the research question.

   a. Not content with posing a question, the researcher now hazards an answer, exhibiting his expectations.

   b. Very little research is totally exploratory.

   c. Generally, the researcher has some idea of what he is going to get.

   d. Prior research and experience has led him to feel that certain outcomes are more likely than others.

3. Null *hypothesis* is a step beyond the research statement.

   a. The null has certain philosophical advantages in the act of statistical testing.

   b. Researchers tend to be cautious and conservative in their statements of conclusions.

      Example: Flat statement: "There is no relationship between . . ."

      Conservative: "I find no substantial reason to doubt that there is a relationship between . . . "

E. EXPLORATION VERSUS CONFIRMATION

1. In *exploratory* research, the researcher is probing relatively new territory, looking for whatever is there.

   Example: A researcher trying to find out the superiority of one of four methods of teaching math: lecture only; class discussion with visual aids; problem solving at a uniform class pace; and problem solving individually paced.

2. If the researcher has no real expectation that any particular method will prove superior, he is essentially *exploring.*

3. In this case, a formal hypothesis is not really necessary.

4. If statistical testing of results indicates the likelihood that one method may be clearly superior to the others, then the researcher may wish to set up a more tightly controlled *confirmation* experiment with hypothesis.

5. The use of formal hypotheses tends to focus the researcher's efforts and attention on a rather narrow and central scope of endeavor.

   a. Their use is valid in verification research where possible outcomes have already been identified and extraneous variables controlled.

   b. Their use could be a serious limiting factor to a researcher who is interested in anything that may result from the experiment or survey.

E. SUMMARY

1. A hypothesis is a quasi-conjectural statement about a population.

    a. If a researcher can test an entire population, he can wipe out all doubts.

2. If a researcher cannot measure the entire population, then he must settle for a random sample of this population.

    a. In this case, he cannot prove his contention absolutely.

    b. He can only make a statistical inference, the strength of which will vary with the controls employed in his sampling procedure.

3. If a researcher cannot even sample the entire population, then he will find himself working with a sample of a sub-population.

    a. Once again he can only make a statistical inference, and that about the sub-population.

    b. Any statement about the entire population will be nothing more than what might be termed a "statistical conjecture."

4. Since a hypothesis is a statement about a population, it should not be worded with vocabulary that applies to sample testing.

    Example: Proper: There is no difference between male and female undergraduate college students in their attitudes toward corporal punishment.

    Improper: There *will* be no *significant* difference between male and female undergraduate college students in their attitudes toward corporal punishment.

There is a twofold offense in the second hypothesis:

    a. "Will be" implies a predictor statement about the research sample.

    b. "Significant" is a specific statistical word referring to sample testing.

Both are inappropriate for a statement about a population.

5. A hypothesis is a statement about a population. A research question is generally sufficient for an exploratory study. The null hypothesis lends itself to statistical testing.

REFERENCES

Best, J. W. *Research in Education.* Englewood Cliffs, NJ: Prentice-Hall, Inc., 1970.

Borg, W. R. *Educational Research: An Introduction.* New York, NY: David McKay Company, Inc., 1963.

Van Dalen, D. B. *Understanding Educational Research: An Introduction.* New York, NY: McGraw-Hill Book Company, 1966.

UNIT V

DATA GATHERING TECHNIQUES

	Page
THE QUESTIONNAIRE	117
THE INTERVIEW	127
PARTICIPANT OBSERVATION	137
UNOBTRUSIVE MEASURES	143
OBSERVATION TECHNIQUES	151
MULTIPLE CRITERION MEASURES FOR EVALUATION OF SCHOOL PROGRAMS	155

THE QUESTIONNAIRE

The questionnaire is a device for securing responses to statements or questions by using a form which the respondents fill out as they provide opinions or factual information. The questionnaire is the most widely used technique of gathering data in the field of educational research and evaluation. Since criticisms of questionnaire studies usually relate to incompetent or careless construction, it is most fitting that investigators be thoroughly familiar with the principles delineating valid questionnaires.

Questionnaire design cannot be taught from books; every research or evaluation study presents new and different problems. A text can only hope to prevent the investigator from falling into some of the worst pitfalls and to give practical, do-it-yourself information that will point the way out of difficulties. This unit attempts to do just that—furnish guidelines and checklists that will assist the practitioner develop a valid and reliable questionnaire.

A. WHEN IS A QUESTIONNAIRE APPROPRIATE?

1. The researcher should be familiar with the full range of possible responses to all of his questions.

2. The researcher believes that the respondents will be willing to accept the relatively passive role of indicating which of the potential answers apply to him.

3. The information sought is sufficiently structured so that it can be explained by means of a printed question or statement.

4. The researcher should be content with the data received without having to follow up with additional questions or interviews.

5. The questionnaire is particularly appropriate when the sample being surveyed is rather large (over 100) and is widely scattered geographically.

6. The selected sample should be sufficiently homogeneous for the researcher to believe that he will have a useful and usable set of data even if the proportion of responses drops below 50 percent.

B. ADVANTAGES OF THE QUESTIONNAIRE

1. Relatively inexpensive mass coverage of potential respondents.

    a. Questionnaires can facilitate collection of data from a large sample in a rather short period of time.

2. Complete standardization of instructions to which the respondents are exposed.

    a. All respondents are exposed to the same items in the same format.

3. The ability to include all response formats provides the researcher with great flexibility in the nature of the information sought.

4. The researcher is able to cover a large geographical area quickly, efficiently, and economically.

5. Well-constructed questionnaires are not as likely to be contaminated by those conducting the research.

6. The questionnaire is usually more convenient for the respondent to complete, particularly in reference to place, time of day, and length of time needed.

7. Questionnaires allow the respondent to supply data not normally accessible to the researcher: private thoughts, feelings, actions, emotion-laden material, etc.

8. Since questionnaires are self-administered, the accompanying anonymity can bring about more honest responses.

C. DISADVANTAGES OF THE QUESTIONNAIRE

1. Ways to check for validity and reliability are limited.

2. The length and breadth of items on a questionnaire are limited.

    a. Excessive probing, resulting in a lengthy questionnaire, might seriously affect the validity of the instrument.

3. The possibility of a low response rate and the concomitant lack of validity is always a threat.

4. Individuals' hostility towards questionnaires might affect their validity.

5. The researcher is not sure who fills out the mailed questionnaire.

6. Questions must be stated so that their intent is clear without additional clarification and interpretation.

7. The validity of the response often depends on the respondent's real

awareness of self and on his "accurate memory" when dealing with past events (selective recall).

8. The responses often tell more about the respondent than about the topic under consideration.

9. Responses may be biased—the respondent can skip questions and come back to them later.

D. VALIDITY AND RELIABILITY

1. Reliability: a reliable questionnaire item is one that consistently conveys the same meaning to those who read it.
   a. Some experience could alter one's knowledge and/or attitude.
   b. Question—wording could cause some bias.

2. Validity: the validity of a questionnaire item is concerned with whether or not the item elicits the intended information.
   a. It is essential that the respondent understands and responds to the question/statement as it is understood by the individual conducting the investigation.

3. Have a number of internal checks to ascertain reliability—vary the way the same question is asked.

E. BASIC STEPS OF QUESTIONNAIRE DEVELOPMENT (Cox, 1976)

1. Defining the problem.
   a. The researcher must have the goals and objectives of the study clearly identified before beginning construction of the questionnaire.
   b. The questionnaire is a means to an end—decisions and/or conclusions will result from the data gathered.

2. Determining the contents.
   a. The researcher should be well acquainted with the topic of the study, having reviewed the literature and consulted with experts.
   b. The responses (open-ended) given to various areas under scrutiny by a small sample will furnish data from which objective-type items may be derived.

3. Identifying and categorizing respondents.
   a. The investigator should be certain that the study and the questionnaire items are appropriate for the respondents.
   b. The questionnaire should collect only enough biographic/demographic data to make conclusions meaningful.

    c. Although anonymity and confidentiality must be preserved, the investigator must determine how returned questionnaires will be identified (initials, color coding, pictures, underscoring, etc.).

4. Developing items and format.

    a. Details of format, English usage, printing, etc., can serve to give the respondents a favorable/unfavorable first impression.

    b. Write as many questions as you need at first; then edit, cut, combine, discard until you have questions that will provide all the data needed while taking no longer than ten minutes for parents and fifteen minutes for school staff (in general) to complete.

5. Writing directions.

    a. Besides being expertly designed, the questionnaire must be skillfully introduced and justified.

    b. An introduction should state the reason for the questionnaire and explain how the information will be analyzed.

    c. Give sample, specific, and complete instructions.

       (1) Explain the way an answer should be recorded, such as, "Check the answer you prefer."

       (2) More rarely, simple definitions will be offered (e.g., "In counting the number of rooms in your home, include the kitchen but do not count the bathroom").

6. Ensuring response.

    a. The researcher must make detailed plans to cover all aspects of guaranteeing maximum returns: from simplicity of format to contacting those from whom no response came.

F. THE LETTER OF TRANSMITTAL (COVER LETTER)

1. This letter should contain a clear, brief, yet adequate statement of the purpose and value of the questionnaire.

2. It should be addressed to the respondent specifically.

3. It should provide good reason for the respondent to reply.

4. It should involve the respondent in a constructive and appealing way.

5. The respondent's professional responsibility, intellectual curiosity, personal worth, etc., are typical of response appeals.

6. The letter should establish a reasonable, but firm, return date.

7. An offer to send the respondent a report of the findings is often effective, though it carries with it the ethical responsibility to honor such a pledge.

8. The use of a letterhead, signature, and organizational endorsements lend prestige and official status to the letter.

9. The letter should guarantee anonymity and confidentiality.

10. Each letter should be signed individually by the researcher.

11. The researcher should include a stamped, self-addressed envelope for the return of the instrument.

G. THE QUESTIONNAIRE ITSELF

1. The *title.*

   a. Avoid titling the document "Questionnaire."

   b. Try to give the document a title based on content.

   c. A clever, but general title can be followed by a more formal, complete subtitle.

   Example   A Matter of Opinion
                (1981-82 school year staff reaction)

   Example: Changing the Subject
                (Evaluation of English 103
                    Revised Class Content)

   Note: Be sure that the "clever" title does not become a biased one. The title, "Let's Change the Subject," could very well predispose the respondents to favoring change.

2. The *introduction.*

   a. Since the administrator alone usually receives the letter of transmittal, it is useful to preface the instrument itself with a short introduction aimed at the respondents themselves.

   b. The introduction should be short, to the point, and intriguing. The respondent will anticipate the same being true of the document which follows it.

   c. This introduction should tell what the form is, why it was created, why the recipient's response is important, how long the form will take to complete, and when and how the respondent will be informed of plans or decisions made.

3. The *design.*

   a. Make sure the questionnaire is as eye appealing as possible.

   b. Make it easy to complete.

   c. Do not crowd items—remember to have some "white space."

   d. Place the title on the first page in bold print.

   e. Include brief and clear instructions, which should be printed in bold face or italics or "boxed off."

    f. Reproduce the questionnaire as professionally as possible.

    g. Do not feel restricted to the use of black ink on white paper; colored paper/inks and artful reproductions increase the appeal of the instrument and the rate of return.

    h. Design must meet the double goal of the questionnaire: provide the respondent with the ability to answer in a way which reasonably reflects his answer, and provides the researcher with the data he needs in the form in which he needs them.

    i. Sometimes the use of drawings and art work increases the appeal of the instrument and/or letter of transmittal.

4. Questionnaire *items*.

    a. Be sure that the respondent realizes whether a factual answer or an opinion is desired.

    b. Write words out completely; all abbreviations may not be known to all respondents.

    c. Make response options mutually exclusive and independent.

    d. Balance all scales used in the response options by having an equal number of options on each side of the middle position.

    e. There is wide disagreement over a neutral response category; the researcher may choose to furnish such an option or not depending on the nature of his study.

    f. Make provision for the systematic quantification of responses.

    g. Include an "Other" category, where appropriate.

5. Improving questionnaire *items*.

    a. Define or qualify terms that could easily be misinterpreted.

      Example: What is the value of your house? (Assessed value? Market value?)

    b. Be careful in using descriptive adjectives and adverbs that have no agreed-upon meaning.

      Example: Frequently, occasionally, rarely, etc.

    c. Beware of double negatives.

      Example: Are you opposed to not requiring students to shower after gym?

    d. Be careful of inadequate alternatives.

      Example: Married? Yes _____ No _____ (Widowed? Separated? Divorced?)

    e. Ask for only one item of information per statement.

        Example: Do you believe that gifted students should be placed in special groups for instructional purposes and assigned to separate schools?

f. Underline a word if you wish to indicate special emphasis.

g. When asking for ratings or comparisons, a point of reference is needed.

        Example: How would you rate this professor's teaching? (In reference to what? Other professors in this school? Other professors that you have had?)

            _____ Superior   _____ Average   _____ Below Average

h. Design items that will give a complete response.

        Example: Do you read the *Indianapolis Star?* (What sections? How often?)

i. Phrase items so that they are appropriate for all respondents.

        Example: What is your monthly teaching salary? Paid on a twelve-month, ten-month, nine-month basis? (Three items really needed here.)

j. Use an introductory phrase, such as "Now, to help classify your answers statistically, may I ask you a few questions about you and your family?" at the beginning of the questionnaire prior to asking classification questions.

6. Things to avoid in constructing questionnaire items.

   a. Avoid unwarranted assumptions.

        Example: Are you satisfied with the salary raise that you received last year?

   b. Avoid response set by varying items so that positive answers are not always at the same end of the scale.

   c. Avoid the use of more than one adjective per item.

   d. Avoid technical and colloquial expressions.

   e. Avoid words which convey different meanings but are used interchangeably.

        Example: Could, might, would, etc.

   f. Avoid phrasing items in such a way that they suggest a positive or negative response.

        Example: Isn't it true that abortion laws should be changed?

   g. Avoid the use of "If yes, then . . . " items.

        Example: Are you married? _____ Yes _____ No; if yes, is your wife employed? _____ Yes _____ No.

Is your wife employed? _____ Yes _____ No
_____ Not applicable

7. *Item* sequence.

 a. Are later responses biased by early items?

 b. Does the questionnaire start off with easy, impersonal items?

 c. Are leading questions asked?

 d. Is there a logical, efficient sequencing of items, as from general to specific?

 e. Are filter items used when needed?

 f. Could ordinal or nominal data be collected as interval data?

 g. Are major issues covered thoroughly, while minor issues are passed over quickly?

 h. Are items with similar content grouped logically?

H. ESTABLISHING AND KEEPING RAPPORT

1. Is the questionnaire easy to answer?

2. Is little respondent time involved?

3. Is the layout attractive?

4. Is the questionnaire introduced with an explanation of purpose, sponsorship, method of respondent selection, anonymity, and confidentiality?

5. Are directions and possible options repeated on each page of the instrument?

6. Has the investigator avoided words that may have emotional overtones, such as abortion, divorce, freedom, sex, etc.

I. PRETESTING THE QUESTIONNAIRE

1. Select a sample of individuals who are representative of the population toward which the questionnaire is eventually intended.

2. Administer the pretest under conditions comparable to those anticipated in the final study.

3. Provide space on the trial questionnaire for the respondents to make reactions and suggested changes.

4. Check the percentage of responses as an estimate of what will occur in the final run.

 a. Then examine the returned trial questionnaires for trouble signs: items left blank or yielding no useful information, misinterpretations, ambiguities.

 b. Check written comments for similar indications.

5. Wait seven or eight days and administer the questionnaire to the same group once more.

   a. Match the questionnaires by individual respondent and determine the consistency with which individuals responded to each item.

   b. Naturally, there will be a memory factor to consider—individuals will remember some items and will not reread them closely.

   c. If an individual responds to an item in dissimilar ways on the two occasions, there may be something wrong with the item that muddles interpretation.

   d. These efforts to perfect the instrument will not be overly taxing since the pretest sample will consist of ten to twenty respondents.

6. Make appropriate additions, deletions, and modifications to the questionnaire to yield the information desired.

J. FOLLOW-UP ACTIVITIES

1. If the percentage of returns is below 70 percent, the validity of conclusions will be threatened.

   a. In any response of less than 70 percent, there is a problem of generalizability.

2. Before proceeding, try to determine if the nonrespondents are different from the respondents in some systematic way.

   a. Phone or personally interview the sub-sample of non-respondents, using questionnaire items.

   b. If responses are generally the same, it may be assumed that the group that responded is representative of the parent population and that results are generalizable.

3. Should the need for additional data become apparent, a postcard reminder should be sent to the nonrespondent group.

4. If sufficient returns are not forthcoming, a follow-up letter should be sent to the nonrespondents.

   a. This letter should assume the tone that the respondent had intended to return the questionnaire but had perhaps overlooked doing so.

   b. It should reaffirm the importance of the study and the value of the individual's contribution to this important study.

   c. Once again, include a self-addressed, stamped envelope.

5. The Research Division of the N.E.A. reports the following results in return rates of questionnaires:

   a. The first follow-up effort, mailed approximately fifteen days after the original mailing, will result in a 63.4 percent return.

   b. The second follow-up effort, mailed approximately twenty-five days after the original mailing, will result in an 83.6 percent return.

   c. The third follow-up effort, mailed approximately thirty-five days after the original mailing, will result in a 96.8 percent return.

6. All follow-up returns should be codified as such: first follow-up, second follow-up, etc.

   a. The response pattern of these follow-up groups should be determined and compared with the original returns for abnormalities.

   b. Severe discrepancies between the response pattern of the original group and that of subsequent follow-up groups should be noted before entering follow-up data into the overall data pool.

   c. In fact, severe discrepancies would argue against adding these follow-up data to the original data pool.

REFERENCES

Berdie, D. R. and Anderson, J. F. *Questionnaires: Design and Use.* New Jersey: The Scarecrow Press, Inc., 1974.

Brown, F. G. *Principles of Educational and Psychological Testing.* New York, NY: Holt, Rinehart and Winston, 1976.

Cox, J. *Basics of Questionnaire Construction in Educational Settings.* Los Angeles, CA: Office of the Los Angeles County Superintendent of Schools, 1976.

Dillman, D. "Increasing Mail Questionnaire Response in Large Samples of the General Public," *Public Opinion Quarterly,* 36, (Summer 1972) 254-7.

Fox, D. J. *The Research Process in Education.* New York, NY: Holt, Rinehart and Winston, 1969.

Isaac, S. and Michael, W. *Handbook in Research and Evaluation.* San Diego, CA: Robert R. Knapp, 1971.

Oppenheim, A. N. *Questionnaire Design and Attitude Measurement.* New York, NY: Basic Books, Inc., 1966.

Webb, E. J., Campbell, D., Schwartz, R. D., and Sechrest, L. *Unobtrusive Measures: Nonreactive Research in the Social Sciences.* Chicago, IL: Rand McNally, 1972.

THE INTERVIEW

The data-gathering process called the interview may be conceptualized as a two-person process through which usable information relative to the respondent's knowledge and/or feelings about a topic is obtained. The interview is then a specialized pattern of verbal interaction initiated for a special pupose, and focuses on some specific content area, with the subsequent elimination of extraneous material.

The information-getting interview includes a broad range of material. Information is not equated with fact finding alone, but is also concerned with attitudes, values, feelings, hopes, plans, and descriptions which the respondents might entertain about some topic. As such, the interview is not restricted to what is objective, superficial, or easy to verbalize; rather, this process includes attempts to get at partially formed attitudes and at private, seldom verbalized feelings. The interviewer may even contribute, through his techniques and the relationship he establishes, to the respondent's ability to formulate and pull together his attitudes regarding the topic under discussion.

The interview can produce valid and reliable data when one is knowledgeable of what the entire process entails. Even though the interview is, in essence, an art involving a multitude of unpredictable human transactions, one presumes that, like any other art, interviewing expertise can be acquired through training and experience by persons who have a knack for talking comfortably in a wide variety of circumstances.

A. CONCEPTS VITAL FOR INTERVIEWING

1. Attributes: the aspects of the topic under consideration.
2. Comparative judgment: operations used to analyze the above aspects.
3. Index numbers: the mathematical treatment of the resulting data.
4. Validity/reliability: of the constructs and numbers that emerge.
5. Estimation of error.

B. BASIC CHARACTERISTICS OF THE INTERVIEW

1. Ability to uncover dimensions of human functioning and educational processes not revealed by other techniques.

2. Ability to gather and analyze large amounts of data from small samples of respondents.

3. Reminder to educational practitioners of the many dimensions of the educational enterprise other than day-to-day preoccupations.

4. Transactions produced are closely observed and controlled.

5. No attempt is made to change the respondent.

C. STRENGTHS OF THE INTERVIEW

1. Assists the investigator to probe to a greater depth, thereby gaining more complete data.

2. Permits the investigator to establish and maintain rapport with the respondent.

3. Assures the interviewer of the effectiveness of his communication through opportunities to clarify equivocal questions.

4. Makes possible the eliciting of information from children and/or people with limited literacy.

5. Makes possible the gaining of confidential and unplanned additional information.

6. Affords opportunity to gain response to questions (95 percent versus a 40 percent on questionnaires).

7. Is flexible and adaptable to individual situations.

8. Allows insights into true feelings of the interviewee—through glimpses of his gestures, tone of voice, etc.

D. WEAKNESSES OF THE INTERVIEW

1. Exacts great toll in time and personnel.

2. Requires highly trained and skilled interviewers.

3. Is open to many biases—interviewer's, respondent's, situational, etc.

4. Presents problems in quantification and the recording of responses.

5. Restricts sample size because of time and money limitations.

E. TYPES OF INTERVIEWS

1. *Unstructured:* totally free response pattern, allowing the respondent freedom to express himself in his own way and in his own time.

    a. This type is most open to biases in interpretation of responses.

      b. The information elicited is usually of a personal and potentially threatening nature.

      c. It necessitates a coding operation which will assist in placing responses into logical categories (measureable).

      d. This type calls for great skill on the part of the interviewer.

2. *Semistructured:* limited free response, curtailing the breadth and time of the response.

3. *Semistructured:* built around a set of basic questions from which the interviewer may branch off to pursue responses in depth.

      a. The interviewer is given the opportunity to explore equivocal and hidden relationships that might go undetected in a more structured response mode.

4. *Structured:* respondent can select his responses only from those provided by the interviewer.

      a. Interviewer is limited as to the extent of clarification he may offer.

      b. This type is most appropriate when information is needed from all respondents and when it readily fits a structured sequence.

      c. It assumes that the interviewer has included questions covering all possible relevant responses.

5. *Structured:* structured response with free option—usually a category called "Other" at the end of a list of possible responses.

6. *Structured:* interviews with schedule.

      a. This involves the administration of a printed list of questions, or schedules, in the presence of the investigator who gives directions and answers questions.

F. GROUP INTERVIEWS

1. Interviewing two to six respondents at a time can be viewed as a savings in time and money.

2. Such grouping can stimulate new ideas among participants.

3. Through the direct observation of the group process, the interviewer can gain an understanding of the temporal dynamics of attitudes and opinions.

4. This technique can promote greater spontaneity and candor.

      a. Respondents who are uncomfortable and inarticulate in the presence of the interviewer may open up in a group interview.

      b. Such respondents are supported by their fellows and can direct their comments as much to each other as to the figure in control.

    5. Such interviews can serve as useful, scouting devices preliminary to construction of a formal, personal interview study.

G. TELEPHONE INTERVIEWS

    1. Interview travel is eliminated and costs reduced.

    2. Interviewer works from the comfort of the home, thereby heightening the quality of his performance.

    3. The anonymity provided by the telephone might promote greater candor than would a face-to-face interview.

        a. Sensitive information appears to be accessible by phone.

    4. Not everyone has a phone—a limitation in random sampling.

        a. More unlisted numbers are used each day.

        b. It is not clear to what extent unlisted numbers differ from others.

    5. All together, telephone surveys are liable to greater inaccuracies than person-to-person interviews.

H. INTERVIEWING AS A QUESTIONING METHOD

    1. Questioning as a *process:* looks for answers to provide a basis for a deeper feeling or attitude the respondent has.

        a. The answer itself is not important, but rather what it implies.

    2. Questioning as a *method of inquiry:* looks for surface information that is provided by responses that are of direct interest in and of themselves.

I. STAGES OF DEVELOPING THE INTERVIEW

    1. Preparing the interview questions.

    2. Pilot study.

    3. Conducting the interview.

    4. Organizing the data.

Note: Each of the above stages is treated separately in the following sections.

J. PREPARING THE INTERVIEW QUESTIONS

    1. Review of the literature: to insure an understanding and clarification of the problem.

        a. To insure representative questions.

        b. To identify appropriate population sample.

        c. To specify variables involved.

        d. To determine method of quantifying data.

e. To determine the nature/type of interview to use.

2. Relevance of interview questions.

   a. Relevance establishes a frame of reference.

   b. Relevance helps establish rapport with the respondent as well as supply information associated with the solution of the problem.

3. Form of the interview question.

   a. Direct/indirect: interview may utilize both.

   b. Specific/nonspecific: although structured and semi-structured interviews use more of the former, the latter may also be used.

   c. Fact/opinion: choice is determined by kind of data desired.

   d. Statement/question: the former offers control; the latter, open-endedness.

   e. Predetermined/response-keyed: with the former, the interviewee answers every question; with the latter, he can skip questions, depending upon his answers to key questions.

4. Content of the interview question.

   a. Points to be explored are arranged in sequence to allow the natural flow of the interview from point to point.

   b. Where appropriate, begin with factual questions and simple topics.

   c. Complex questions should come later.

   d. Questions which might embarrass or cause hostility, however slight, or which could affect the replies to subsequent questions, should be left till near the end of the interview.

   e. After sequence has been decided, frame specific questions in precise wording, using unambiguous language that the interviewee can readily understand.

   f. The language level of both vocabulary and sentence structure should be compatible with the level of understanding of the interviewees.

   g. The interviewer should not try to communicate as the respondent does; such an attempt could decrease the respondent's respect for him in his role as interviewer.

   h. Avoid leading questions which might suggest that a particular response is expected.

   i. Utilize rating scales, check lists, or attitude scales, where appropriate, either as the interview instrument itself, or as the basis upon which interview questions are developed.

K. THE PILOT STUDY

1. Use sample similar to the one constituting the interview sample.

2. Record answers from pilot sample as fully as possible.

   a. Tape and/or video-tape recordings of pilot sessions are highly desirable.

3. At conclusion of pilot, omissions are corrected, the order of questions is revised, where necessary, and word changes to remove ambiguities are made.

4. Prompts and probes are inserted where necessary to press main questions (prompts) or to clarify replies (probes).

   Example:

   Question: "What kind of teacher evaluation is most appropriate?"

   Prompt: If the interviewee says, "It depends on the purpose of the evaluation," say, "Assume that the purpose is improvement of instruction rather than accountability."

   Probe: If the interviewee says, "A method that rates the teacher's ability to meet individual needs of children," say "What rating technique would accomplish this?"

5. Review the responses in the pilot run.

   a. Determine the range of answers to be expected.

   b. Prepare the schedule to include a system of recording and classifying answers; for example, the more frequent responses can be listed on the schedule so that during the interview responses can be circled.

   c. The layout of the schedule should permit easy checking of answers, for example, in a margin.

L. CONDUCTING THE INTERVIEW

1. The cardinal rule of interviewing is to follow the "script" in a natural manner.

2. Take whatever steps deemed necessary to establish rapport: joke, indirect approach, etc.

   a. Begin scheduled questions when the respondent is judged "ready," a procedure followed to "warm up" TV audiences before a taping begins.

   b. Affective variables—dress, voice, place, time, etc.—must be considered and controlled as much as possible.

   c. A freer response can be expected if the respondent is interviewed privately.

    d. Distinguish between and assure respondent of confidentiality/ anonymity, as appropriate.

3. Recording data during unstructured and semistructured interviews is always a problem and can be approached in several ways.

    a. Trust one's memory to record after the interview: highly unreliable.

    b. Record by hand during the interview may slow the pace unnecessarily or cause the interviewer to be more selective in the kind and amount of data he records. This approach is distracting to the respondent and a waste of time.

    c. Recording of responses by a third party who positions himself unobtrusively in the interview area. This approach can be distracting to the respondent and affect the validity of his answers.

    d. Audio-tape recording yields greater coverage and recall and frees the interviewer to focus directly on the respondent's "body language." The threat associated with this approach becomes less likely as tape recorders become more widely used in one's everyday needs.

    e. Video taping interview sessions would be highly desirable. More complete coverage, total recall of responses, and an accurate record of "body language".would be insured. Few interviewers have access to such equipment, which could be threatening to the respondent because of attendant noise, lighting, site of interview, etc.

M. ORGANIZING THE DATA

1. Reliability and validity are enhanced if one person conducts the interview and records his observations, and a second person interprets these data.

    a. Gaps in information can be obtained by an additional contact or follow-up phone call.

2. Unstructured interviews are valuable for initial interviewing, but since results resist quantification, this method should be avoided at the final data-collection stage.

3. Possible response modes should lend themselves to the nature and purpose of the interview and the intended use of the data collected.

    a. Fill-in: limited range of answers are available, but elicits nominal data.

    b. Checklist: responses are more controlled than in fill-in and provide nominal data also.

    c. Scaled responses.

Highly usable   Slightly usable

d. Ranking responses: answers represent a continuum and are easily quantified.

e. Categorical responses: Yes/No; True/False, etc., are easily quantified.

f. Tabular responses: useful for quantifying complex data.

   Example: What is your proficiency level in each language that you speak?

	Excellent	Good	Fair	Poor
First Language				
Second Language				

4. Analysis and interpretation of quantified data can be sharpened through use of insights gained through open-ended questions.

5. The investigator can return to the interview to assist him in the interpretation of abnormalities discovered in the quantified data.

   Example: A polarization of responses represented by a bimodal distribution at each end of a scale can be investigated through follow-up interviews with samples of the responding group(s).

REFERENCES

Collins, A. *The Interview: An Educational Research Tool.* Palo Alto, CA: ERIC/IR, 1970.

Dyer, H. S. *The Interview as a Measuring Device in Education.* Princeton, NJ: ERIC/TM, 1976.

Fox, D. J. *The Research Process in Education.* New York, NY: Holt, Rinehart, and Winston, Inc., 1969.

Gorden, R. L. *Interviewing: Strategy, Techniques, and Tactics* (Rev. Ed.). Homewood, IL: The Dorsey Press, 1975.

Isaac, S. and Michael, W. B. *Handbook in Research and Evaluation.* San Diego, CA: Robert R. Knapp, Publisher, 1971.

Kahn, R. L. and Cannell, C. F. *The Dynamics of Interviewing.* New York, NY: John Wiley and Sons, Inc., 1967.

Kerlinger, F. N. *Foundations of Behavioral Research.* New York, NY: Holt, Rinehart, and Winston, Inc., 1973.

Nisbet, J. D. and Entwistle, N. J. *Educational Research Methods.* New York, NY: American Elseview Publishing, 1970.

Tuckman, B. W. *Conducting Educational Research.* New York, NY: Harcourt, Brace, Jovanovich, 1972.

Van Dalen, D. B. and Meyer, W. J. *Understanding Educational Research.* New York, NY: McGraw-Hill, 1966.

Webb, E. J., Campbell, D. T., Schwartz, R. D., and Sechrest, L. *Unobtrusive Measures: Nonreactive Research in the Social Sciences.* Chicago, IL: Rand McNally, 1966.

PARTICIPANT OBSERVATION

Anthropological and sociological research involves the study of a whole human system in its natural setting. Such holistic study attempts to capture and express some of the complexity of human beings and their organizations. As such, participant observation involves a systematic sharing in the life activities and interest of a group of persons.

Participant observation of schools allows an evaluator or researcher to experience a program in depth, to become part of the students and staffs daily lives, to observe behavior as it occurs naturally. Sometimes this approach may be the best way for evaluators to arrive at a relatively complete, comprehensive picture of a program in general—a Gestalt of operations, people, and their interactions. On-site observation permits input of a richness and detail that seldom can be achieved through any secondary source such as test instruments.

A. RATIONALE FOR PARTICIPANT OBSERVATION APPROACH

1. The holistic standpoint includes the belief that human systems tend to develop a characteristic wholeness or integrity.

2. Human systems are not simply a loose collection of traits, wants, reflexes or variables of any sort.

   a. They have a unity that manifests itself in nearly every part.

3. The holist believes not only that wholes exist, but that his account of them should somehow capture and express this holistic quality.

   a. Accompanying this attitude is a feeling that the only instrument that is good enough for studying human beings is man himself.

   b. Only the human observer is perceptive enough to recognize and appreciate the full range of human action.

   c. Only the human thinker is able to draw the proper implications from the complex data coming from human systems.

B. NATURE OF THE PARTICIPANT OBSERVATION APPROACH

1. Participant observers study a process or an environment by observing and experiencing it in depth.

2. They attempt to understand individuals or groups by becoming part of those individuals' or groups' daily lives.

3. Data are collected by direct contact with real life situations and by observing behaviors as they occur naturally.

   a. It permits more or less continuous observations of a program's staff and/or service recipients *in situ* while the program is in operation.

   b. For this reason, it may be particularly useful for program planning and improvement.

4. Since it allows the researcher to observe behavior as it occurs, he does not depend solely on an informant's accuracy to describe his own or others' actions.

   a. Off-hand remarks give insights not normally gathered.

C. ADVANTAGES OF THE PARTICIPANT OBSERVATION APPROACH

1. The spontaneous quality of the data gathered is particularly useful in potentially sensitive areas such as staff complaints about program operations, etc.

   a. This approach can provide a check against systematic distortion in the perception of interviewees.

2. Participant observers are not likely to be misled by dissembling respondents.

   a. They can use their knowledge of specific incidents to face an issue and assist a respondent to clarify what he means.

3. The participant observer learns the meanings of the respondents' words and speech patterns with great precision.

4. The participant observer approach is particularly effective when:

   a. The subjects under study are sufficiently different from the usual to warrant this kind of attention.

   b. There is a homogeneous community or group to observe.

   c. The purpose of the study is the understanding of the system of behavior and the interrelationships within it.

5. Participant observation can provide constructive feedback to a program staff that is receptive to such feedback.

   a. The observer can facilitate communication between various components of a program.

b. He can ferret out and invite attention to inefficiencies in program operation.

c. He can then facilitate improvements through consultation or "ombudsmanship."

6. As a rule, participant observation may be most efficient when combined with:

a. Case studies.

b. Pretest and posttest studies and analysis of statistical data.

c. Document analysis.

d. Personal interviews with those whom the participant observer was unable to observe directly.

D. DISADVANTAGES OF THE PARTICIPANT OBSERVATION APPROACH

1. Because the data gathered are the perceptions and reactions of individual observers, quantification and manageable summary may be very difficult.

2. Recording of behaviors and events usually takes place sometime after their occurrence, so that the observer must recreate and rethink what occurred.

a. Although this rechecking may sharpen and refine initial impressions, it can just as easily produce inaccuracies and distortions.

3. There is the possibility that an evaluator who lives with a program staff for a considerable period of time will lose his objectivity and will adopt the biases or perceptual distortions of the program staff.

4. An *identified* participant observer may cause program staff to behave atypically or unnaturally.

5. An *unidentified* observer probably will have access only to information that routinely is disseminated to someone not in a formal role position.

6. This technique is usually very time consuming and expensive and requires a trained observer to carry out observations efficiently.

E. MAJOR STYLES OF PARTICIPANT OBSERVERS

1. *Complete participant:* the evaluator presents himself as a legitimate program staff member; his assessment function is kept secret and he is assigned a regular role in the program's operation.

a. This method avoids staff anxiety and hostility about the evaluator's presence, so that they will go about their work activities freely and naturally.

b. Evaluator's task is complicated by the fact that he must satisfactorily perform his cover role as well as carry out the "undercover" assessment.

c. If he is a lower-level staff member or a service recipient, his freedom of movement with the program may be severely constrained.

d. Some questions may arise about the ethics of complete deception.

2. *Participant as observer:* in this role, the evaluator's real purpose is not concealed from the program staff, but they are made subordinate to his formal function as a member of the program.

a. The evaluator is usually accepted by program staff as one of them since he spends most of his time on actual program activities.

3. *Observer as participant:* here the importance of the two roles is reversed; the evaluator's known and primary function is to assess the program.

a. The evaluator may participate creatively in program activities.

b. He is clearly an outsider.

4. *Complete observer:* the evaluator has no formal participative role in program operations, but is, more or less, a silent observer of the same program activities.

a. Opportunities for feedback with program staff are restricted.

b. In-depth observation is still possible.

F. SOME STEPS IN THE PARTICIPANT OBSERVER PROCESS

1. Prior preparation.

a. Become acquainted with the school(s) to be visited.

b. Review the literature relevant to the type of program to be observed.

c. Have an agreed role which is accepted by those with whom the observer will work; the role selected will define, to some extent, the way others respond to the observer and the type of things the observer will be free to assess.

d. Prepare checklists of things for which to look, which, however, should be amenable to change.

e. Anticipate and prepare for role conflict: acceptance as a co-teacher in informal discussions in the faculty lounge, but rejection as an evaluator observing classroom activities.

2. In the school(s).

a. Scheduled activity connected with formal task.

b. Collect routine data.

      c. Carry out unobtrusive open and structured interviews.

      d. When permitted by designated role, become totally involved in the school community.

      e. Note taking can be in public, when appropriate or accepted; write up field notes each evening.

3. Gradual development of themes.

      a. As observation progresses, themes are identified, then interpreted.

      b. Each interpretation is tested, refined, reinterpreted, expanded, discarded, if necessary, as new data are observed and collected.

4. Data gathering methods.

      a. Interviews: open and/or structured.

      b. Documents: memos, reports, official records, minutes of various meetings, school census data, etc.

      c. Observations: single or multiple observers, volunteers from the community, photographs, recordings, etc.

      d. Tests, questionnaires, sociogram analyses, mappings, counts, etc.

      e. Excellent information comes from informal, casual comments or from an analysis of omissions from official records.

      f. Contextual validity, or dependability, can be tested by accepting possible bias in all data collected and by cross checking sources.

      g. Multiple examples of evidence from different sources reinforce each discovered theme.

5. Organization of themes into an overall model.

      a. The system model, developed from themes and interpretations, both describes and explains activity of the whole system, but is rarely completely finished.

      b. Through the process of constructing the model, missing connections are revealed, thereby necessitating a return for more data.

      c. There is constant circular movement between stages, a flexibility, from the model back to themes and interpretations, to the data, back to the model, etc.

      d. The problem of how to present material collected involves careful selection, but writing up the study or evaluation can be highly creative.

      e. Participant observation reports have strong appeal because of their informal style, their personal, down-to-earth descriptions, and the multiple hypotheses they generate for further study.

REFERENCES

Adams, R. N. and Preiss, J. J. (Eds.). *Human Organization Research.* Homewood, IL: Dorsey Press, 1960.

Hammond, P. E. (Ed.). *Sociologists at Work.* New York, NY: Basic Books, 1964.

Jacobs, G. (Ed.). *The Participant Observer.* New York, NY: G. Braziller, 1970.

UNOBTRUSIVE MEASURES

Today, conclusions drawn in the behavioral sciences rest dominantly upon data which is based on interviews and questionnaires. Too often, the investigator relies upon one of these single, fallible methods. These interviews and questionnaires often intrude as foreign elements into the social setting they would describe. They oftentimes create, as well as measure, attitudes, they elicit atypical roles and responses, their data most often come from those who are accessible and who will cooperate, and the responses obtained are produced in part by dimensions of individual differences irrelevant to the topic at hand.

But the main objection to such data-gathering techniques is that they are used alone. No research method is without bias. Hence, interviews and questionnaires should be supplemented by different methodological weaknesses. The real issue is not one of choosing among individual methods, but rather it is the necessity for using a collection of methods to avoid sharing the same weaknesses. In this unit, various "approximations to knowledge" are presented in light of their unobtrusive effect on subjects participating in research and evaluation studies. Such measures do not require the cooperation of the respondent and do not, themselves, contaminate the response.

A. APPROACHES USED TO ACHIEVE INTERPRETABLE COMPARISONS

1. Experimental design.

    a. These designs are difficult to apply in the behavioral sciences.

    b. Randomization—a difficult condition to obtain—lies at the heart of experimental design.

2. Index numbers.

    a. Indices control sources of variance known to be irrelevant by transformations of raw data and weighted aggregates.

       Example: End-of-the-year bad weather means more unemployment and less retail buying. But holiday gift giving, Christmas bonuses, etc., offset this negative trend.

3. Plausible rival hypotheses.

    a. The more of these that exist, the less valid is the interpretation of accumulated data.

    b. The number of rival hypotheses can be reduced through use of experimental methods, indices, critical reaction of fellow scientists (e.g., those opposing views held by Jenkins and Shockley).

B. VALIDITY

1. Internal validity.

    a. This type validity asks whether a difference exists at all in any given comparison.

    b. It also asks whether or not an apparent difference can be explained away as some measurement artifact.

    c. It also argues that even the appearance of a difference is spurious.

2. External validity.

    a. This type validity directs itself toward the problem of interpreting the difference—the problem of generalizability.

    b. It asks to what other populations, occasions, stimulus objects, and measures may obtained results be applied.

3. The distinction between internal and external validity is illustrated in two uses of randomization.

    a. When the experimentalist in psychology randomly assigns a sample of persons into two or more experimental groups, he is concerned entirely with internal validity—with making it implausible that the luck of the draw produced the resulting differences.

    b. When a sociologist carefully randomizes the selection of respondents so that his sample represents a larger population, representativeness or external validity is involved.

C. SOURCES OF INVALIDITY OF MEASURES

1. Reactive measurement effect: error from the respondent.

    a. Awareness of being tested—the guinea pig effect (e.g., presence of a TV camera with initials NBC, LAPD, etc.).

    b. Role selection: involves not so much inaccuracy, defense, or dishonesty, but rather a specialized selection from among the many "true" selves or "proper" behaviors available in any respondent.

c. If the testing (interview, questionnaire, etc.) is not a normal condition, the experimenter forces upon the subject a role-defining decision: "What kind of person should I be as I answer these questions or do these tasks?"

d. Validity decreases as the role assumed in the research setting varies from the usual role present beyond the research setting.

e. Response to all cues, i.e., the demand characteristics of the experimental situation contributes to role selection.

f. Subjects with little formal schooling are less familiar and less comfortable with testing and are more likely to produce nonrepresentative behaviors.

g. The experimenter may expect the same distortion when the subjects are confronted with new, unexpected, and unfamiliar material.

h. "Expertness" bias: "You have been selected as part of a scientifically selected sample . . . It is important that you answer all items . . . " Such wording results in fewer "don't know" answers.

i. The act of measuring can, of itself, function as a change agent through "practice effects" influence, thereby threatening internal validity.

j. "Preamble effect" creates attitudes which influence responses.

k. Response sets: subjects will more frequently endorse a statement than disagree with its opposite—the acquiescence response set.

l. Subjects consistently manifest preference for strong statements as opposed to moderate or indecisive ones.

m. Sequences of questions asked in very similar format produce stereotyped responses—better to arrange randomly in right-hand, left-hand order.

n. Right-turn bias, placement of exits, fatigue, deadlines, etc., can all complicate erosion, accretion techniques.

2. Reactive measurement effect: influence of the investigator.

a. The race of the investigator (interviewer), his sex, his age can affect respondents' answers.

Example: Younger interviewers receive considerably more "unacceptable" responses than do older persons.

b. Consideration not only to main effects but also to interactions.

Example: Age and sex variables: male interviewers obtain fewer responses than do females, and fewest of all from other males, while female interviewers obtain their highest responses from men, except for young women talking to young men.

Example: Preference for type of waiter in restaurants: men in high-priced establishments; middle-aged as opposed to young women; who gets largest tips?

3. Reactive measurement effect: change in the research instrument.

   a. The instrument is often the researcher, the interviewer, the data gatherer himself.

   b. The data gatherer's skill may increase; he may be better able to establish and maintain rapport with his respondents; perhaps he has better command of the necessary vocabulary.

   c. The data gatherer may become bored or lackadaisical; he may have increasingly strong expectations of what a respondent "means"; he may code differently with practice.

   d. Differences in the instrument (interviewer) may be interpreted as contextual differences.

      Example: Suicides in Prussia jumped 20 percent in 1882-83. This reflected a change in record keeping, not a massive depression within the state (as viewed with the 1929 suicide rate in the United States because of widespread mental depression).

   e. Sometimes, early returns in data influence the analysis of subsequent data.

4. Sampling error.

   a. In public opinion polling, one conceptualizes a "universe" which is represented by the sample polled. However, only certain universes are possible for any given method.

      Example: Interviews in public places exclude 80 percent of the total population.

      Example: In-home interviewing with quota controls and no call-backs excludes 60 percent: 5 percent inaccessible, 25 percent not at home, 25 percent refusals, 5 percent interviewer's reluctance to approach home of extreme wealth or poverty and fourth-floor walkups.

   b. Those who answer doorbells overrepresent the old, the young, or women.

   c. A considerable portion of the populace is functionally illiterate for personality and attitude tests developed on college/university populations.

d. Differential volunteering: subject dependent, the curious, the exhibitionist, and the succorant are likely to overpopulate any sample of volunteers.

e. Faulty reliance on representation through automobile registration and the telephone directory will result in faulty representation: the above exclude 30 percent of the population.

Example: There are more homes with TV sets than with phones or baths.

f. Phone surveys encounter unlisted numbers; a problem which can be offset by random digit dialing; however, this will cause a tenfold increase in cost as will three (at least) callbacks for no answers.

5. Population stability.

a. Time element: population will differ on dry days as opposed to wet (snowy) days, spring as opposed to winter weather, by day of the week.

b. Seasonal layoffs, status accorded summer vacations as opposed to winter vacations will affect sample population.

c. Element of geography: region compared to other regions, accessibility of public transportation will affect numbers riding buses as opposed to commuter trains or taxis.

D. SOURCES AND TYPES OF UNOBTRUSIVE MEASURES

When a particular proposition has been confirmed by two or more independent measurement processes, the uncertainty of its interpretation is greatly reduced.

1. Physical records.

a. *Natural erosion:* classic example of determining the most popular exhibit in Chicago's Museum of Science and Industry as indexed by the frequency of replacing vinyl tiles.

(1) This unobtrusive measure was based on records of the museum's maintenance department; hence, two sources to start with.

(2) The question of whether the erosion resulted from a greater number of people viewing the chick-hatching exhibit, or just more foot shuffling by normal groups. This necessitated a head count; hence, a third source.

(3) The wear on library books (corners where pages are turned), compared to circulation rates of same books (see "Date Due" slips) would indicate which books are actually read and not just withdrawn from the library.

b. *Controlled erosion:* involves some intervention by the researcher such as putting actometers on children to measure activity.

  (1) Adapting self-winding watches to actometers is useful for research with children.

  (2) Care to determine whether or not floor tile is coated with a preservative to cover worn grooves (people tend to walk in previously chosen paths), etc., will present misleading data.

c. *Natural accretion:* refers to behavior traces laid down without the intervention of the social scientist.

  (1) Studying the frequencies to which a car's radio was tuned, accumulation of various types of insects smashed onto front of car, help merchants identify most-listened-to stations, most-visited areas, etc.

  (2) Size of clothing most produced (e.g., knights' armor), size of floor areas in old dwellings, etc., can give clues to variations over the years in humans' physical sizes, sizes of families, etc.

d. *Controlled accretion:* refers to behavior traces which involves some intervention on the part of the researcher.

  (1) The glueing together of certain advertisement-carrying pages in a popular magazine, finger and nose smudges on display cases (heights of these smudges can be linked to ages of viewers), gross body movement in an audience, etc., are examples of indirect and unobtrusive data-gathering techniques.

2. Archives: two major biases of this source are selective deposit and selective survival.

  a. Actuarial records: births, deaths, marriages, census, etc.

  b. Large-scale social studies as Masters' study of sex habits, Coleman's study of educational practices, etc.

  c. Voting records of party members, entire political parties, etc., produced a "Loyalty Shift Index" and an "Index of Coalitions."

  d. Mass media are the most easily accessible and massive source: newspapers, radio, TV, songs, speeches, handbooks, photographs, books, etc.

  e. Specific areas within mass media are equally rich in data: weather reports, traffic fatalities, shortages, etc.

  f. Public records: variations in gas pressure, water pressure, etc., can yield evidence of peak use and prevailing weather conditions.

3. Archives (episodic and private records as opposed to public) are more difficult to obtain.

a. Sales records, institutional records, and personal documents are the chief sources.

    (1) These records serve to support observation techniques (e.g., observing alcohol consumption by United Nations delegates, supported by register sales) might give clue to tension within that body.

    (2) Multiple records (e.g., incidence of crashes and height of pilots in Navy jets) gave clues to information concerning size of cockpit, placement of instrument panel, etc.

    (3) Popularity of memorabilia—Kennedy half dollars, commemorative stamp issues (time and nature), autographs, etc., are all good indicators of public opinion and likes.

4. Simple observation.

    a. The observer has no control over the behavior or subject in question, but plays an unobserved, passive, and nonintrusive role.

    b. Participant observer study is exposed to "control effect" and "biased viewpoint effect."

    c. Exterior physical signs: beards, tattooing, clothing, signs, etc.

    d. Expressive movement: facial expressions, finger and hand movements, jiggling, movement by athletes such as dusting with resin bag, knocking dirt from cleats, running to the right (football), etc.

    e. Physical location: proximity to the leader, interrace seating, personal space, turning habits, etc.

    f. Language behavior: subject of conversation, with whom, etc.

    g. Time sampling designs consider duration, degree of sophistication, familiarity with the observer, previous experience in being observed, type of situation, and number of individuals in the situation.

5. Contrived observation: hidden hardware and control.

    a. Today many such devices might be considered an invasion of privacy and have legal complications.

    b. Tape recorders, polygraphs, eye movement and dilation, body movement recorders, etc., are examples of hardware used.

    c. Entrapment: giving subjects opportunities to cheat.

    d. Planned intervention by the observer: "I just got my driver's license . . . ," the deliberate jay walker, etc.

REFERENCES

Adams, R. N. and Preiss, J. J. (Eds.). *Human Organization Research.* Homewood, IL: Dorsey Press, 1960.

Berelson, B. *Content Analysis in Communication Research.* Glencoe, IL: Free Press, 1952.

Campbell, D. T. "The Informant in Quantitative Research," *American Journal of Sociology,* 1955, 60, 339-342.

Webb, E. J., Campbell, D. T., Schwartz, R. D., and Sechrest, L. *Unobtrusive Measures: Nonreactive Research in the Social Sciences.* Chicago, IL: Rand McNally and Company, 1972.

Weiss, D. J. and Davis, R. V. "An Objective Validation of Factual Interview Data," *Journal of Applied Psychology,* 1960, 44, 381-385.

OBSERVATION TECHNIQUES

An observation system is merely a special language for describing the behaviors by which we communicate. We might call such a system a "meta language," that is, a language for talking about language. In order to be useful for describing communication, such a language must be descriptive rather than evaluative, deal with what can be categorized or measured, and must deal with bits of action or behavior, and not global concepts (Simon and Boyer, 1974).

It is only recently that concerted attention has been given to the development of observational systems for the purpose of describing the process of on-going verbal and nonverbal interactive behaviors as they occur and to suggest explicit modifications, where necessary.

A. COMPONENTS OF OBSERVATION SYSTEMS AND INSTRUMENTS

1. Very sophisticated systems with a large number of categories that provide for fine distinctions and much information about the behaviors under scrutiny.

   a. Long training periods are needed.

   b. Difficulty of obtaining 100 percent reliability between/among coders using the system.

2. Systems with few categories which allow only gross distinction and little information about behaviors being investigated.

   a. Little training is needed.

   b. Easy to learn, resulting in greater interobserver reliability.

3. Most systems fall between the above two extremes.

   a. Categories of conceptual importance are selected.

   b. These categories of behaviors are then grouped along some theoretical dimension.

     c. Observers are trained to code behaviors into one of the existing categories, or, in case of nonfit, code them into a miscellaneous category.

B. CLASSES OF BEHAVIOR (Simon and Boyer, 1974)

1. Affective.

     a. Primary focus is on the emotional component of communication.

     b. The "support-reject" dimension focuses on "whole person" behaviors: asking or giving feelings, telling about the self, or supporting/rejecting another person.

     c. The "understanding versus judging" dimension describes reactions to someone's idea: clarify, expand, think through, tell more versus judging the idea.

2. Cognitive.

     a. Primary focus is on the intellectual component of communication.

     b. One main category of cognitive behavior consists of giving data, asking for data, clarifying, defining, and giving opinions.

     c. A second main category attempts to get at some structured analysis of the thought processes themselves.

     d. Cognitive models may be: task analysis models, developmental models, psychometric models, etc. (Thomas, 1972).

3. Procedures, Routine or Control.

     a. These categories focus on what is being talked about.

     b. "Getting ready to work" includes statements about working procedures, behavioral boundaries/limitations, sanctions.

     c. "Working on the content" deals with statements about specifically assigned subject matter.

     d. "Administrative routine" refers to those "nonwork" areas that plague most teachers, including roll call, milk money, etc.

4. Physical Environment.

     a. Such categories describe the physical space where observations are taking place and note specific materials or equipment being used.

     b. Teacher surrogates such as CAI, IPI, Discovery, Inquiry technology are now being considered, as are a great number of media-lecturer surrogates, such as audio and video tapes, motion pictures, TV, etc.

5. Psychomotor.

     a. This category focuses on behaviors by which people communicate when they are not using words: posture, position in relation to others, facial expressions, gestures, etc.

6. Sociological Structure.

   a. This category focuses on who is talking to whom, the role(s) of people being observed, numbers and types—age, gender, race—of people who are interacting, etc.

7. Activity.

   a. These observational systems focus on the activities in which people are engaged: reading, looking at films, hitting someone, etc.

   b. Measurement of infant and small child behaviors normally falls into this category.

8. Other Specialized Systems.

   a. Some single-focus systems have special and, hence, highly delimited foci: teacher role, lesson form and format, subject matter area, spatial relationships of children to teachers, size of pupil groups, speech patterns, etc.

C. CODING UNITS

1. Most systems use specific predetermined categories, such as "teacher asks question," "pupil gives narrow answer," "person leaves the room," etc.

   a. Most of these systems also use a time unit which gives some sense of elapsed time as well as category change in behavior (Flanders, 1966).

   b. Some systems add an additional set of categories to note who is speaking, or to note change of speaker.

   c. Some systems make provision for noting a change in the audience rather than (or in addition to) the speaker.

   d. Some few note a change in topic or content.

   e. Some coding units include: episodes, a complete verbalized thought, occurrence of a specific incident, etc.

2. Rating scales are also used in observational systems.

   a. Such scales do not count behavioral acts, but serve as guides to making judgments about a subject.

   b. Scales vary from indicators of the amount of something (some, few, several, many), or judgments of quality (poor, fair, good, excellent) to hierarchial items that are behaviorally defined (child talks: not at all, seldom, occasionally, constantly).

D. COLLECTION METHODS

1. Virtually all observational systems can be coded from recorded inputs instead of having to use live, on-the-scene recording.

2. Some systems allow the observer to code while being part of the interaction in a natural setting.

3. Some require on-the-scene recording if categories like smell, touch, and heat radiation are to be measured and could not be inferred from audio- or video-tape recordings.

REFERENCES

Flanders, N. A. *Interaction Analysis in the Classroom: A Manual for Observers.* Ann Arbor, MI: School of Education, University of Michigan, 1966.

Simon, A. and Boyer, E. G. (Eds.). *Mirrors for Behavior III: An Anthology of Observation Instruments.* Philadelphia, PA: Research for Better Schools, 1974.

Thomas, J. W. *Varieties of Cognitive Skills: Taxonomies and Models of the Intellect.* Philadelphia, PA: Research for Better Schools, 1972.

MULTIPLE CRITERION MEASURES FOR EVALUATION OF SCHOOL PROGRAMS

An evaluator initiates his strategy by identifying the information he needs in order to answer evaluative questions about the program under consideration. He is then faced with the problems of how further to identify the sources (people, records, etc.) of this information and how to collect it (variables, instrumentation, etc.).

Metfessel and Michael (1967) have assembled a list of measures that concentrate largely on program outcomes and which serve to broaden the evaluator's view of measures that may provide useful evaluation information.

A. **Indicators of Status or Change in Cognitive and Affective Behaviors of Students in Terms of Standardized Measures and Scales.**

   1. Standardized achievement and ability tests, concerned with knowledge, comprehension, understanding, skills, and applications.

   2. Standardized self-inventories designed to yield measures of adjustment, appreciations, attitudes, interests, and temperament.

   3. Standardized rating scales and checklists for judging the quality of products in visual arts, crafts, shop activities, penmanship, letter writing, fashion design, and other activities.

B. **Indicators of Status or Change in Cognitive and Affective Behaviors of Students by Informal or Semiformal Teacher-made Instruments or Devices.**

   1. Interviews: frequencies and measurable levels of responses to formal and informal questions raised in a face-to-face interrogation.

   2. Questionnaires: frequencies of responses to items in an objective format and numbers of responses to categorized responses to open-ended questions.

3. Self-concept perceptions: measures of current status and indices of congruence between real self and ideal self.

4. Self-evaluation measures: student's own reports on his perceived or desired level of achievement, personal and social adjustment, or future academic and vocational plans.

5. Teacher-devised projective devices, such as casting characters in the class play, role playing, and picture interpretation.

6. Teacher-made achievement tests (objective and essay), to determine which specific instructional objectives have been attained.

7. Teacher-made rating scales and checklists for observation of classroom behaviors; performance levels of speech, music and art; creative endeavors, personal and social adjustment, physical well being.

8. Teacher-modified forms of the semantic differential scale.

C. **Indicators of Status or Change in Student Behavior Other Than Those Measured by Tests, Inventories, and Observation Scales in Relation to the Task of Evaluating Objectives of School Programs.**

1. Anecdotal records and case histories: critical incidents noted, including frequencies of behaviors judged to be highly undesirable or highly deserving of commendation.

2. Attendance: frequency and duration when attendance is required or considered optional (as in club meetings, special events, or off-campus activities).

3. Autobiographical data: behaviors reported that could be classified and subsequently assigned judgmental values concerning their appropriateness relative to specific objectives concerned with human development.

4. Citations: commendatory in both formal and informal media or communication such as in the newspaper, television, school assembly, classroom, bulletin board, or elsewhere.

5. Extracurricular activities: frequency or duration of participation in observable behaviors amenable to classification such as taking part in athletic events, charity drives, cultural activities, and numerous service-related avocational endeavors.

6. Grade placement: the success or lack of success in being promoted or retained; number of times accelerated or skipped.

7. Performance: awards, extra credit assignments and associated points earned, numbers of books or other learning materials taken out of the library, products exhibited at competitive events.

8. Recidivism by students: incidents (presence or absence or frequency of occurrence) of a given student's returning to a probationary status,

to a detention facility, or to observable behavior patterns judged to be socially undesirable (intoxicated state, dope addiction, hostile acts, including arrests, sexual deviation).

Other possible indicators include: absences, appointments kept or broken, assignments completed, changes in program or in teacher as requested by student, choices expressed or carried out, disciplinary actions taken, number of dropouts, elected positions held, grade point average, grouping, homework assignments, leisure activities, library card possessed, numbers of units or courses carried, peer group participation, recommendations of others, referrals, skills, social mobility, tardiness, transiency, transfers and withdrawals from school.

D. **Indicators of Status or Change in Cognitive and Affective Behaviors of Teachers and Other School Personnel in Relation to the Evaluation of School Programs.**

1. Attendance: frequency of, at professional meetings or at in-service training programs, institutes, summer schools, colleges and universities (for advanced training) from which inferences can be drawn regarding the professional person's desire to improve his competence.

2. Mail: frequency of positive and negative statements in written correspondence about teachers, counselors, administrators, and other personnel.

3. Memberships, including elective positions held in professional and community organizations: frequency and duration of association.

4. Rating scales and checklists (e.g., graphic rating scales of the semantic differential) of teachers' behaviors in the classroom or of administrators' behavior in the school setting regarding changes of behavior in professional competence, skills, attitudes, adjustment, interests, and work efficiency.

5. Records and reporting procedures practiced by administrators, counselors, and teachers: judgments of adequacy by outside consultants.

Other possible indicators include: articles written; grade point average; load carried by teacher; moonlighting; nominations by peers, students, administrators, or parents for outstanding service and/or professional competencies; termination; request for transfers.

E. **Indicators of Community Behaviors in Relation to the Evaluation of School Programs.**

1. Alumni participation: numbers of visitations; extent of involvement in PTA activities; amount of support of a tangible (financial) or a service nature to a continuing school program or activity; attendance at

special school events, at meetings of the board of education, or at other group activities by parents.

2. Conferences between parent-teacher, parent-counselor, parent-administrator sought by parents: frequency of.

3. Letters (mail): frequency of requests for information, materials and services; frequency of praiseworthy or critical comments about school programs and services and about personnel participating in them.

4. Participant analysis of alumni: determination of locale of graduates, occupation, affiliation with particular institutions, or outside agencies.

5. Parental response to letters and report cards upon written or oral request by school personnel: frequency of compliance by parents.

6. Telephone calls from parents, alumni, and from personnel in communications media (e.g., newspaper reports): frequency, duration, and quantifiable judgments about statements monitored from telephone conversations.

7. Interview data.

REFERENCES

Metfessel, N. S. and Michael, W. B. "A Paradigm Involving Multiple Criterion Measures for the Evaluation of Effectiveness of School Programs," *Educational and Psychological Measurement,* 1967, 27, 931-943.

UNIT VI

DEVELOPING SCALES

	Page
THURSTONE OR EQUAL INTERVAL SCALE	161
LIKERT SCALE	165
GUTTMAN SCALE OR SCALOGRAM ANALYSIS	169
SEMANTIC DIFFERENTIAL	173
NORM-REFERENCED MEASUREMENTS VERSUS CRITERION-REFERENCED MEASUREMENTS	177

THURSTONE OR
EQUAL INTERVAL SCALE

Thurstone's scale of equal appearing intervals was developed in the early '30s by L. L. Thurstone. It is moderately easy to construct, and has a comparatively high reliability with some difficulty in reproducibility. Two important features of the scale are the equal appearing intervals and 'the use of judges in the construction phase. There are four steps in the design of the Thurstone Scale.

A. STEPS IN SCALE CONSTRUCTION

1. Composition of an item pool.

   a. Compose a set of declarative unidimensional statements. There should be as many statements as possible but not to exceed 250 items. Ideally, items should number between 100 and 200 items.

   b. The strength of the items is unimportant.

   c. There is no need for positive and negative statements.

   d. Variations of the same statement(s) may be included.

   e. Reproduce the declarative unidimensional statements on cards. Cards measuring 3 x 5 inches is recommended. A set of cards should be made for each judge to be utilized.

2. Selection of judges and judging.

   a. Define the population on which the research is to be carried out.

   b. Select from a similar population judges who will assist in judging the items developed above.

   c. The number of judges is not set; however, it is suggested that as many as possible be acquired. Judges numbering from forty to sixty is acceptable. Multiples of ten is recommended for ease in scoring later.

    d. The judges should be totally informed as to their role in the development of the scale. They should be informed also about what the scale is to measure.

    e. Request the judges to place each item on the cards given them along a hypothetical scale. The scale generally has eleven sections ranging from "most unfavorable" (a score of one) to "most favorable" (a score of eleven). The spaces between sections are considered equal. No item is to be placed between sections.

    f. The task of each judge is to place each item in one of the eleven sections. No item is to be placed between sections.

    g. Each judge is given a complete set of item cards which have been randomized by item. The item cards given the judges should be randomly selected from the differing packs of cards. The judges then begin to place each card in a particular space according to his feelings towards the item. The judge uses his subjective feelings to place the cards.

3. Scoring the judgments or computation of the interval scale.

    a. Assemble all the judgments for each statement or item.

    b. The distribution for each statement is considered in order to reduce the number of statements. If the distribution is spread over several sections and there is no pyramiding of placement frequencies, the item is considered too ambiguous and is discarded. The ideal statement would be one in which all the judges placed it in one section.

    c. The semi-interquartile for each item is calculated. This necessitates the calculation of median scores. The median for each item is calculated using the section numbers as the basis for calculation.

    d. The item value is determined by calculating the median score for the placement frequencies of the judges. The median score is then placed on the section number. This section number then becomes the item value. See example below.

    e. Decide how long the scale is going to be and how many items. Twenty to twenty-five items is acceptable. A longer or shorter scale may be used and is acceptable.

    f. After the size of the scale is determined, select at equal intervals, or as closely as possible, the number of items needed; i.e., a twenty item scale would be ideally made of items with item values of 1.0, 1.5, 2.0, 2.5 . . . 9.5, 10.0, and 10.5.

    g. Parallel forms can be constructed by choosing other items with the same item value. The validity will be nearly equal.

h. When item values are the same and it is decided which item is to be used, the "Q-score" is utilized. The formula for the "Q-score" is: $Q = \frac{1}{2}$ (3rd quartile − 1st quartile). Use the items with the best (i.e., smallest) "Q-score."

Example:

Section No.	Frequency	Percentage	Median
5	0	0%	
6	0	0%	
7	6	12%	
8	19	38%	8.5
9	17	34%	
10	8	16%	
11	0	0%	

The item value for this item is 8.5 and the Q-score is 1.0.

4. Preparation for administration and scoring.

   a. Once the items have been selected from the larger pool of items, they should be placed randomly on a test sheet without their item (scaled) values.

   b. Next to each item should be provided a space for the respondent to agree or disagree with the statement.

   c. Scoring is carried out by marking those items the respondent agreed with, looking up the item scaled value for each item, and determining the median score value for these items. The median score value for the items agreed with becomes the scale score for that respondent.

B. CONCERNS

1. Moderately easy to construct.
2. Has a high reliability.
3. Parallel forms can easily be constructed.
4. Reproducibility is difficult.
5. Simple computations are involved.
6. Locating judges representative of the population is difficult.
7. Unidimensional items are difficult to construct.
8. Only *equal appearing* data is collected.

REFERENCES

Oppenheim, A. N. *Questionnaire Design and Attitude Measurement.* New York, NY: Basic Books, Inc., 1966.

Shaw, M. E. and Wright, J. M. *Scales for the Measurement of Attitudes.* New York, NY: McGraw-Hill, 1967.

Thurstone, L. L. and Chave, E. J. *The Measurement of Attitudes.* Chicago, IL: University of Chicago Press, 1929.

LIKERT SCALE

The Likert scale developed by Rensis Likert is easier and more simply designed than the other scales of attitude measurement. The Likert scale is concerned with the unidimensionality (making sure all items measure the same thing) of an attitude and does away with the use of judges used in other scale construction by having each respondent place himself on a continuum for an attitude item. There are six steps in the construction of the Likert Scale for Attitude Measurement.

A. STEPS IN SCALE CONSTRUCTION

1. Composition of an item pool.

   a. Compose a set of fifty to one hundred declarative unidimensional statements; these statements need not concern themselves with any factor except unidimensionality (i.e., "Policemen are honest," "My parents are fair in their judgments," "My teachers are my friends," etc.).

   b. The strength of the items is unimportant.

   c. There should be equally appearing positive and negative statements. These should appear randomly on the scale.

   d. Variations of the same statement(s) may be included. The above statement, "Policemen are honest," could be varied to read, "Policemen concern themselves with abiding by the law," or "I could trust a policeman with my money."

   e. The number of statements is left open and the number of negative and positive statements should be about equal. This holds true in the final form of the scale when the number of items is reduced to twenty to forty items.

2. Selection of response choices.

    a. It is necessary to select a set of response choices. Research has shown that a response set of five or seven gives the maximum data.

    b. Traditionally, the response choices have been: strongly agree, agree, no opinion (uncertain), disagree, and strongly disagree. Alternatives of these choices could be: strongly approve, approve, undecided, disapprove, and strongly disapprove; or, strongly agree, agree, mildly agree, no opinion (uncertain), mildly disagree, disagree, strongly disagree.

    c. Care should be taken to choose those responses which will give the respondent the easiest choice and will produce maximum data.

    d. The response choices must be appropriate for the statements appearing on the scale.

3. Preparation of test for developmental administration.

    a. All items developed should be placed on the test sheet in random order. The use of a table of random numbers is recommended.

    b. The response choices that have been chosen should be placed to the right (some recommend to the left) of the test items.

    c. The instructions for completing the scale should be placed at the top of the first page or on a covering page. They should be clearly stated. It should be strongly stated that the respondent SHOULD NOT OMIT ANY ITEM.

    d. Sufficient time should be allowed for the completion of the scale. Time is not a factor.

    e. The format of the scale is important. Every item should be easy to read and easy to respond to. The use of wide margins on all sides is highly recommended.

    f. It is important in research that a high percentage of the completed scales be returned for scoring. This percentage should be established before the scale is administered. The literature supports a return percentage of 62 percent or higher. When attempts are made to raise the percentage of return, care should be taken to establish that there are no differences in response patterns in the varying groups.

Example Format:

	Strongly Agree	Agree	No Opinion	Disagree	Strongly disagree
1. Policemen are honest.	—	—	—	—	—

2. My teachers are my friends.   —   —   —   —   —

3. My parents are fair in their
judgments.   —   —   —   —   —

4. Definition of a developmental sample.

    a. A sample population of 100 to 250 should be determined.

    b. This sample should represent the population upon which the final scale will be given after its development.

5. Scoring.

    a. Each record of each respondent must be scored.

    b. Assign a value to each of the response choices. The values of 1, 2, 3, 4, and 5 are recommended when using the five-choice response set. This assignment must be consistent throughout the scale.

    c. On the negative items, the values *must* be reversed. It cannot be overly emphasized how important this is. It should be done at the very beginning of the scale scoring. All negative statements, therefore, should have the reverse value assignment of those positive statements.

    d. Decide whether the high score represents a favorable attitude or an unfavorable attitude. This decision, too, must be made before scoring begins. If it is decided that 5 is a favorable attitude, then the scoring procedure is begun by giving all "strongly agree" responses a value of 4, all "no opinion" (uncertain) responses a value of 3, etc.

    e. The score for each respondent is obtained by adding the values of those items checked. If a respondent omits an item, the value is 0. Once a total is obtained, it is divided by the number of items that were responded to. This will give a score between 5 and 1.

    f. If the score is 3.1 or more, with a high score being favorable, it can be said that the individual has a positive attitude. If the score is 2.9 or less, a negative attitude exists. If a score of 3.0 is obtained, it is said that the respondent has a neutral attitude.

6. Final scale development.

    a. Item analysis should be carried out to determine the external and internal validity. Factor analysis is most reliable and is a statistically sound technique.

    b. Select from the original items twenty to forty statements which are most sound statistically. There should not be more than forty items on the scale. If there are more, the response/return rate may not be as high as desired.

    c. Prepare the final scale by following the concepts presented above.

Administer the final scale to the research population.

d. Scoring on the final scale is carried out as described above also. Care should be taken in dealing with the positive and negative items.

B. CONCERNS

1. The Likert scale is easy to construct.
2. It has a moderate reliability in the two-forms, split-halves, and test-retest formats.
3. Associated areas of an attitude can be explored.
4. Simple computations are involved.
5. Moderately easy to score.
6. Unidimensional items are difficult to construct.
7. Only nonparametric statistics can be applied to the scores.
8. Individual scores are superior to the group score. Individuals can be discussed in more detail than can the group.
9. Reproducibility is nearly impossible.

REFERENCES

Likert, R. "A Technique for the Measurement of Attitude Scales," *Archives of Psychology,* No. 140, 1932.

Oppenheim, A. N. *Questionnaire Design and Attitude Measurement.* New York, NY: Basic Books, Inc., 1966.

Shaw, M. E. and Wright, J. M. *Scales for the Measurement of Attitudes.* New York, NY: McGraw-Hill, 1967.

GUTTMAN SCALE OR
SCALOGRAM ANALYSIS

The Guttman Method of Scale Analysis, developed by Louis Guttman, is more complicated than either the Likert or Thurstone scales. The construction is difficult. The scale is based on the concept that a scale property is ordinal and cumulative; e.g., addition, multiplication, and the extraction of square roots are arithmetical operations ordered according to their cumulative degree of difficulty. If the scale has been constructed based upon social distance, then the individual's score will indicate the degree to which he accepts the attitude or concept being tested.

A. STEPS IN SCALE CONSTRUCTION

1. Composition of an item pool.

   a. A "universe" of descriptive statements is composed.

   b. Those items which are thought to best represent the attitude being measured are selected out.

   c. These items are placed on a sheet with a two-choice option: Yes, No.

2. Trial testing.

   a. The items are administered to a sample population similar to the population on which the research is being conducted.

   b. All items are scored by a predetermined method. The researcher sets the method before administering the test.

   c. A score is determined for each respondent. Generally, a score is obtained by adding up the number of positive answers.

3. Scaling.

   a. A chart is constructed showing the item across the top and the respondents down the right side. This and the following examples are given by Oppenheim. This procedure enables the researcher to see how the responses have deviated from the ideal scale pattern.

Respondent	Item 1	Item 2	Item 3	Item 4	Item 5	Item 6	Item 7	Item 8	Score
1	yes	yes	yes	yes	yes	- - -	yes	- - -	6
2	yes	- - -	- - -	- - -	yes	- - -	yes	yes	4
3	yes	yes	- - -	- - -	yes	- - -	yes	yes	5
4	- - -	- - -	- - -	- - -	yes	- - -	yes	- - -	2
5	yes	- - -	- - -	- - -	yes	- - -	yes	- - -	3
6	yes	- - -	- - -	- - -	yes	- - -	yes	yes	4
7	yes	yes	- - -	yes	yes	yes	yes	yes	7
8	yes	- - -	- - -	yes	yes	- - -	yes	- - -	4
9	yes	yes	- - -	yes	yes	yes	yes	yes	7
10	yes	yes	- - -	yes	yes	- - -	yes	yes	6
11	- - -	- - -	- - -	- - -	- - -	- - -	- - -	yes	1
12	- - -	- - -	- - -	- - -	- - -	- - -	yes	- - -	1
13	yes	yes	- - -	yes	yes	- - -	yes	yes	6
14	yes	- - -	- - -	- - -	yes	- - -	yes	yes	4
15	yes	- - -	- - -	- - -	yes	- - -	yes	- - -	3

b. After each respondent has been given a score, the chart is rearranged. The respondents are ranked and the highest score(s) are placed at the top. The item response is left unchanged. In the chart below, respondents 7 and 9 received a score of 7, missing item 3.

Respondent	Item 1	Item 2	Item 3	Item 4	Item 5	Item 6	Item 7	Item 8	Score
7	yes	yes	- - -	yes	yes	yes	yes	yes	7
9	yes	yes	- - -	yes	yes	yes	yes	yes	7
10	yes	yes	- - -	yes	yes	- - -	yes	yes	6
1	yes	yes	yes	yes	yes	- - -	yes	- - -	6
13	yes	yes	- - -	yes	yes	- - -	yes	yes	6
3	yes	yes	- - -	- - -	yes	- - -	yes	yes	5
2	yes	- - -	- - -	- - -	yes	- - -	yes	yes	4
6	yes	- - -	- - -	- - -	yes	- - -	yes	yes	4
8	yes	- - -	- - -,	yes	yes	- - -	yes	- - -	4
14	yes	- - -	- - -	- - -	yes	- - -	yes	yes	4
5	yes	- - -	- - -	- - -	yes	- - -	yes	- - -	3
15	yes	- - -	- - -	- - -	yes	- - -	yes	- - -	3
4	- - -	- - -	- - -	- - -	yes	- - -	yes	- - -	2
11	- - -	- - -	- - -	- - -	- - -	- - -	- - -	yes	1
12	- - -	- - -	- - -	- - -	- - -	- - -	yes	- - -	1
	12	6	1	6	13	2	14	9	

c. After each respondent has been ranked, the items are rearranged so that the first column is the item with the greatest number of "yes" responses, the second column is the second greatest number of positive responses, etc. The chart below illustrates this with item 7 receiving the greatest number; item 5, the second greatest, etc. Note that the "respondent" column is unchanged from the chart above.

Respondent	Item 7	Item 5	Item 1	Item 8	Item 2	Item 4	Item 6	Item 3	Score
7	yes	yes	yes	yes	yes	yes	yes	- - -	7
9	yes	yes	yes	yes	yes	yes	yes	- - -	7
10	yes	yes	yes	yes	yes	yes	- - -	- - -	6
1	yes	yes	yes	- - -	yes	yes	- - -	yes	6
13	yes	yes	yes	yes	yes	yes	- - -	- - -	6
3	yes	yes	yes	yes	yes	- - -	- - -	- - -	5
2	yes	yes	yes	yes	- - -	- - -	- - -	- - -	4
6	yes	yes	yes	yes	- - -	- - -	- - -	- - -	4
8	yes	yes	yes	- - -	- - -	yes	- - -	- - -	4
14	yes	yes	yes	yes	- - -	- - -	- - -	- - -	4
5	yes	yes	yes	- - -	- - -	- - -	- - -	- - -	3
15	yes	yes	yes	- - -	- - -	- - -	- - -	- - -	3
4	yes	yes	- - -	- - -	- - -	- - -	- - -	- - -	2
11	- - -	- - -	- - -	yes	- - -	- - -	- - -	- - -	1
12	yes	- - -	- - -	- - -	- - -	- - -	- - -	- - -	1

Note in the above chart that a triangular pattern is produced. Respondents 1, 8, and 11 keep the reproducibility from being perfect.

4. Computation of the index of responsibility.

   a. This index is computed to determine whether those marking the responses that should indicate the quality most strongly are consistently among those with highest total scores.

   b. The formula for computing this index is:

   $$R = 1 - \frac{\text{number of errors}}{\text{number of responses}}$$

   R = the index of reproducibility

   number of errors = the number of errors within the scale; i.e., whether it is due to a wrong answer outside the triangle or a blank within the triangle. See item 8, which has three errors.

   number of responses = the number of items multiplied by the number of respondents.

   c. If the index of reproducibility falls below 0.9, then the scale should be considered unsatisfactory.

     d. The above procedure is simplified if there are multiples of ten in the respondents and the items.

B. CONCERNS.

1. Reaching a satisfactory criterion of scalability is difficult.
2. Even when a high index of reproducibility is achieved, it is not certain whether all items are measuring the same attitude.
3. The selection of good items is difficult.
4. It is difficult to construct.
5. Scoring is easy.
6. It is very time consuming.
7. It is not recommended for research studies.

REFERENCES

Guilford, J. P. *Psychometric Methods.* New York, NY: McGraw-Hill, 1954.

Oppenheim, A. N. *Questionnaire Design and Attitude Measurement.* New York, NY: Basic Books, Inc., 1966.

Shaw, M. E. and Wright, J. M. *Scales for the Measurement of Attitudes.* New York, NY: McGraw-Hill, 1967.

Sidowski, J. B. (Ed.). *Experimental Methods and Instrumentation in Psychology.* New York, NY: McGraw-Hill, 1966.

Stouffer, S. A. (Ed.). *Measurement and Prediction.* Princeton, NJ: Princeton University Press, 1950.

SEMANTIC DIFFERENTIAL

The Semantic Differential was the outgrowth of diverse experimentation that began with investigation of color-music synesthesia. Osgood (1957) and his associates followed with a series of research programs substantiating generalized interrelationships between/among color, adjectives, and graphic visual representations which quite evidently exist even between diverse cultures.

Osgood intended to measure the psychological or connotative meaning of concepts as points in semantic space, "a region of some unknown dimensionality and Euclidean in character." His semantic scales, composed of a set of bipolar adjectives, constituted a linear function that passed through the origin of that space.

A. EARLY DEVELOPMENT.

1. An initial list of adjectives was determined by orally presenting forty nouns from the Kint-Rosanoff list as stimuli to 200 undergraduate students.

   a. The subjects were instructed to write the first descriptive adjective that came to mind.

   b. Definitions of the dimensions of semantic space were accomplished by factor analysis (determined by the number of orthogonal dimensions that could reasonably be extracted).

   c. The *first* rotation of the adjective responses yielded responses of an "evaluative" nature (most sensitive indicator of change).

   d. The *second* rotation identifed a clustering of adjectives which were labeled "potency."

   e. The *third* produced an adjective list identifed as "activity."

   f. The *fourth* rotation accounted for less than 2 percent of the variance.

B. **THE SEMANTIC DIFFERENTIAL IS A METHOD FOR MEASURING THE MEANING OF CONCEPTS.**

1. It is used to measure objectively the semantic properties of words and concepts in a tri-dimensional (concept, scale, subject) space.

2. More commonly, it is used as an attitude scale, usually restricting its focus to the affective domain and/or evaluative dimension.

3. Meaning is assessed by the set of rating scores assigned by the subject.

   a. A number of nonparametric tests of significance can be used to interpret scores.

C. **SCALE CONSTRUCTION.**

1. Select the concepts to be evaluated in terms of their semantic or attitudinal properties.

   a. These concepts should be relevant to the topic under investigation.

   b. These concepts should be sensitive to differences and/or similarities among the comparison groups.

   c. If several concepts have to be rated, it is best to have a separate rating sheet for each one.

   d. Thus, the same set of scales can be given over and over, each time with a different concept heading the page.

2. Select the bipolar adjective pairs that anchor the scale.

   a. These bipolar adjectives should be opposites or near opposites.

   b. This "oppositeness" should *not* be accomplished merely through the use of negative prefixes; e.g., "imaginative-unimaginative," "fair-unfair," "practical-impractical," etc.

   c. Some extremes have *more* than one opposite; e.g., "sweet-bitter," or "sweet-sour."

   d. Some extremes have *no* opposites; e.g., "burning," so that instead of having two extremes, we really have but one extreme and a neutral end, "not burning."

   e. Where attitudes are concerned, adjective pairs with high evaluative loadings are often appropriate, although the selection of polar adjectives simply on their "face value" for a given situation is perfectly acceptable.

3. Arrange the bipolar adjectives so that the positive, active, or potent end of the scale is randomly placed in a left- or right-hand position.

   a. This random arrangement will serve to nullify or prevent mindsets from developing.

b. The scale itself should consist of a series of undefined scale positions, which, for practical purposes, is not less than five nor more than nine steps, *seven* being the optimal number.

Example:

INDEPENDENT STUDY

good	__ :	__ :	__ :	__ :	__ :	__ :	__	bad
active	__ :	__ :	__ :	__ :	__ :	__ :	__	passive
dislike	__ :	__ :	__ :	__ :	__ :	__ :	__	like
weak	__ :	__ :	__ :	__ :	__ :	__ :	__	strong
heavy	__ :	__ :	__ :	__ :	__ :	__ :	__	light
useless	__ :	__ :	__ :	__ :	__ :	__ :	__	useful
excited	__ :	__ :	__ :	__ :	__ :	__ :	__	calm
dull	__ :	__ :	__ :	__ :	__ :	__ :	__	sharp

The subjects would place an "X" somewhere along each of the seven-position scales according to their perceptions of it or how they feel towards it at that moment.

D. ANALYSIS AND EVALUATION.

1. By converting the scale positions to numerical values, various statistical assessments can be made.

good $\underline{7} : \underline{6} : \underline{5} : \underline{4} : \underline{3} : \underline{2} : \underline{1}$ bad

OR

good $\underline{1} : \underline{2} : \underline{3} : \underline{4} : \underline{5} : \underline{6} : \underline{7}$ bad

a. It does not matter whether a high score or a low score represents positive or negative feelings towards the concepts.

b. *Consistency* in the scoring arrangements is necessary.

2. Since the concepts, the scales, and the subjects are the three main sources of variance, the scores can be analyzed for congruence and/or discrepancy among concepts, scales, and subjects in any combination.

3. The more commonly used statistical analyses applied to scores are:

a. The D statistic, which is determined by taking the difference between scores of concepts for each factor, squaring the difference, summing the squares, and computing the square root of the sum.

b. The t-test, or Median test, of significance for individual or summed scales.

c. The *profile analysis,* using the sign test to determine if the profiles generated by two groups tend to stand apart or overlap.

E. CAUTIONS.

1. The assumption of equality of intervals, both within each scale and between different scales must be reviewed.

2. The respondents' scores might reflect either theoretical or utilitarian biases (sometimes both are found).

3. The difficulty of using the same scales to measure respondents' attitudes towards various concepts; e.g., can we apply "calm-excited" to certain foods?

4. The scale's factorial composition is often not available.

REFERENCES

Isaac, S. and Michael, W. *Handbook in Research and Evaluation.* San Diego, CA: Robert R. Knapp, 1971.

Jenkins, J. J., Russell, W. A., and Suci, G. J. "An Atlas of Semantic Profiles for 360 Words," *The American Journal of Psychology,* 71, (1958), 688-699.

Osgood, C. E., Suci, G. J., and Tannenbaum, P. H. *The Measurement of Meaning.* Urbana, IL: University of Illinois Press, 1957.

Shaw, M. E. and Wright, J. M. *Scales for the Measurement of Attitudes.* New York, NY: McGraw-Hill Book Company, 1967.

Snider, J. G. and Osgood, C. E. (Eds.). *Semantic Differential Techniques.* Chicago, IL: Aldine, 1969.

NORM-REFERENCED MEASUREMENTS VERSUS CRITERION-REFERENCED MEASUREMENTS

In recent years, there has been increasing debate over the differences between *norm-referenced measurement* and *criterion-referenced measurement*. Both have their place within the educational domain; however, the decision of when either or neither of these measurement techniques is appropriate must be based upon a clear understanding of their functions, attributes, and weaknesses. Basically, the main difference between norm-referenced measurement and criterion-referenced measurement can be described in the example of a foot race: if a runner's performance is judged in relation to others (e.g., "He came in first!"), that is norm-referenced measurement; whereas, when a runner's performance is examined in relation to a predetermined behavioral domain (e.g., "At the completion of a three-week runner's training clinic, a runner will be able to complete a measured mile in under six minutes."), that is criterion-referenced measurement.

The two kinds of tests represent different views of the measurement process. Norm-referenced tests assume a trait (e.g., reading skill) that all individuals in the population have but in different amounts. The test is aimed at discovering who has more or less of that trait. Criterion-referenced tests do not assume a knowledge continuum; instead, a desired behavior is carefully described and the assessment aims at discovering whether or not an individual has achieved the objective. Also, it is important to keep in mind that these two measurement techniques—while very popularly used in school settings today—are not the only means of assessing student achievement or aptitude.

A. An awareness of the *purposes of achievement testing* is essential ground-work for understanding the why of norm-referenced and criterion-referenced measurement. Shoemaker (1975) lists ten.

  1. To determine the pupil's level of academic development in order to better adapt materials and instructional procedures to his needs and abilities.

  2. To diagnose specific qualitative strengths and weaknesses in a pupil's academic development.

  3. To indicate the extent to which individual pupils have specific skills and abilities needed to begin instruction or to proceed to the next step in the instructional sequence.

  4. To provide information useful in making administrative decisions in grouping or programming to better provide for individual differences.

  5. To diagnose strengths and weaknesses in group performance (class, building, or system) which have implications for change in curriculum, instructional procedures, or emphasis.

  6. To determine relative effectiveness of alternative methods of instruction and the conditions which determine effectiveness of various procedures.

  7. To assess effects of experimentation and innovation.

  8. To monitor constantly the progress of individual students with respect to specific behavioral objectives in order to make immediate instructional decisions.

  9. To monitor constantly the effectiveness of instructional procedures in order to modify them as the need arises.

  10. To provide a model for the pupil to show what is expected of him and to provide feedback which will indicate progress toward goals which are suitable for him.

B. *Definitions* of norm-referenced test and criterion-referenced test.

  1. Norm-referenced tests (Sax, 1975) are "designed to determine an individual's relative standing in comparison with an internal or external norm group."

     Example: A school board wishes to know how the reading performance of children within their district compares with that of other school districts in the same state and the nation.

2. Criterion-referenced tests (Popham, 1978) are "used to ascertain an individual's status with respect to a well-defined behavioral domain."

   Example: A federal aviation licensing agency wishes to determine if an individual has acquired the skills necessary to safely land a passenger jet.

C. *Characteristics common to both* norm-referenced and criterion-referenced and criterion-referenced measurement.

   1. Can be achievement tests.
   2. Can be used for educational assessment and evaluation.
   3. Aimed at assessing instructional objectives.
   4. Both may have norms, a specific criterion level designated as indicative of mastery, and can be standardized.
   5. Administration and scoring are standardized.
   6. Extreme care is required in writing test items.
   7. Historically long-known methods for measurement.

D. Characteristics associated with norm-referenced measurement.

   1. Principal purpose is to discriminate among individuals.
   2. Demonstrates that an individual has more or less knowledge (interest, ability, etc.) than others of a reference group.
   3. Surveys *general* skills and knowledge, common to many educational programs.
   4. Performance is summarized in a distribution of scores, typically highest to lowest.
   5. A raw score in isolation has no meaning (only meaningful by comparison with other scores).
   6. Items selected for their ability to maximize the observing of individual differences.
   7. The distribution of scores is summarized into a *normative scale* to describe relative incidence of success of the reference population.
   8. Often called "standardized" tests. (Note: The ambiguity of the term "standardized" makes it impossible to exclude all criterion-referenced measurement from the term.)

9. Cannot be used as a criterion-referenced test.

10. Test, by itself, is usually not sensitive to differences in treatments.

11. Generally requires an extended interval between testings if done on a pretest and posttest basis.

12. Cannot provide a clear picture of what specifically a student does know.

13. Not sensitive to specific educational objectives; rather, measures broad program goals.

14. Wide variety of options for reporting scores (e.g., raw scores, percentiles, grade level equivalents, etc.).

15. Reliability less vulnerable to external factors (e.g., memory, learning interference, etc.) than for CRT.

16. Reliability established most often by using test-retest or split-half method.

17. Validity concerns include: content validity, construct validity, and, to a lesser degree, criterion-related validity.

18. Test construction includes establishing a *discrimination index* in order to determine the items that contribute to producing overall response variance (e.g., including the items that were most often answered correctly by those who did well on the test and answered incorrectly by those who did badly on the total test).

E. Characteristics associated with criterion-referenced measurement.

1. Compares individual student performance with a level of performance he is expected to achieve.

2. Measures a carefully defined domain of behaviors.

3. Gained popularity in 1960s as an alternative measurement technique to NRT for assessing programmed learning and teaching machines.

4. Little attention paid to content validity, but much to criterion-related validity.

5. An individual's performance has meaning by itself (e.g., no comparison with others' performance is necessary).

6. Aimed at producing an exact description of an individual's performance.

7. Test items may be randomly selected from items that describe a specific domain of behavioral performances.

8. Aimed at providing information about conditions or treatments which produce a specific behavior.

9. Sensitive to differences in treatments (e.g., the test should be much easier for those who have completed the treatment.

10. Designed to discriminate among treatments by analyzing group differences.

11. Sometimes called *objectives-referenced tests.*

12. Often the score is simply the number of objectives attained.

F. Weaknesses of norm-referenced measurement.

1. Broad, general nature of NRTs may make inferences about program effects suspect (e.g., mismatches between what is tested and what is taught).

2. Very difficult technical problems in test development that can lead to elimination of important test items and inclusion of misleading or irrelevant items.

3. Possible cultural bias inherent in tests.

4. Tendency of many users to misinterpret or "overinterpret" (place too much importance on test results) an individual's performance.

5. Test often not helpful in diagnosing how to improve instruction.

6. Test may foster inappropriate competition.

G. Weaknesses of criterion-referenced measurement.

1. Test offers no clues for determining the appropriateness of the objectives that are assessed.

2. Test is often not helpful in determining how effective one program is over another.

3. Apparent ease of construction is deceptive, and, therefore, "unthought-out" CRTs abound in schools today.

4. In some situations (e.g., IQ), no clear behavioral domain exists.

5. The number of items needed to appropriately assess a specific behavioral domain is unknown.

6. Does not discriminate among individuals.

7. Tests do not lend themselves to conventional test statistics.

8. Scoring—which often involves arbitrarily setting minimum limits to indicate objective attainment—is difficult to justify.

Table 1

Characteristic Similarities and Differences Between Norm-Referenced and Criterion-Referenced Achievement Tests

Norm-Referenced Tests	Criterion-Referenced Tests
Content Specifications	
1. Topics outlined and weighted according to importance; number of items per topic is directly proportional to importance.	1. Topics broken down into specific educational objectives; number of items per objective is usually constant. In any case, all objectives are equally represented since each has its own score.
2. Both omission of important content and inclusion of unimportant content are serious flaws that distort meaning of score.	2. Omission of important topics reduces overall value of instrument but does not affect meaning of scores. Unimportant objectives can be ignored.
3. Test usually covers broadly defined educational goals that represent the most widely adopted school curricula.	3. Test covers a set of specific educational objectives.
4. Altering a test to fit a specific local curriculum is very difficult; it is usually easier to build such a test from scratch.	4. The set of objectives used may be easily selected or modified to fit local curricula.
Item Writing Specifications	
1. Items are usually written to learning objectives which represent a sample of those relevant to the goals being measured. Each goal is systematically sampled but objectives are not.	1. Items are written to learning objectives: each objective is systematically sampled.
2. Single items often require knowledge of several aspects of the content.	2. Items refer only to the objective to which they are written.
Desirable Item Characteristics	
The best items are those that:	The best items are those that:
1. discriminate well between those who score high and those who score low on the test,	1. discriminate between those who have and have not had effective instruction to that objective.

Norm-Referenced Tests (con't.)	Criterion-Referenced Tests (con't.)
2. show growth from grade to grade,	2. show mastery immediately after the objective has been achieved.
3. are about midrange in difficulty (but some items at each extreme are also desirable).	3. have preinstruction difficulties approaching 0 (almost all get them wrong) and postinstruction difficulties approaching 1 (almost all get them right).

Administration

1. Standardized conditions of administration are essential, including control of time (sometimes tests are speeded but not always).	1. More latitude in conditions is permissible. Control of time is rarely appropriate (unless speed is part of task).
2. Parts cannot be omitted without damage to meaning of total.	2. Parts can be omitted at will since there is no total score.

Scores

1. Raw scores rarely have much direct meaning.	1. Raw scores have some direct meaning about achievement of the objective being measured.
2. Measurement places person on hypothetical scale of amount of trait.	2. Measurement refers to scales based on visible performance.
3. Scale usually established by norms (comparative performances).	3. Scale is usually established by judgment and convention concerning adequate and inadequate performance but norms may exist and help.
4. Derived scores are used such as standard scores, percentile ranks, grade equivalent scores.	4. Scores used are number right, and categories such as mastery and nonmastery.
5. Score reports usually imply value; i.e., performance was good or poor.	5. Score reports are less well adapted to making conclusions about the quality of student or program performance.
6. All items contribute to part and total scores.	6. Each objective has its own score; meaningful total scores are usually not possible.

Norm-Referenced Tests (con't.)

Score Distributions

1. Score distributions that are approximately normal are desirable; e.g.:

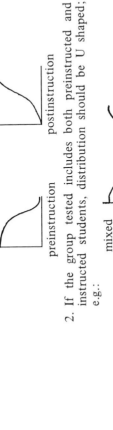

Score

0

Reliability

1. Test-retest coefficients should be high for each score.
2. Internal consistency coefficients should be substantial for each score.

Content Validity

1. Content coverage and emphasis should be judged adequate.
2. Fit of items to their intended content category is a matter of judgment.

Criterion-Referenced Tests (con't.)

1. Score distributions that are skewed are desirable; e.g.:

preinstruction   postinstruction

2. If the group tested includes both preinstructed and instructed students, distribution should be U shaped; e.g.:

mixed

1. Test-retest coefficients should be high for each objective in a mixed sample (as above).
2. Internal consistency coefficients should be high for each objective in a mixed sample.

1. Adequacy of coverage of behavior specified by objective should be adequate.
2. Fit of items to their intended content category is a matter of judgment.

Norm-Referenced Tests (con't.)

Criterion-Referenced Tests (con't.)

Construct Validity

1. Scores show growth during years of school attendance.

2. Scores show greatest growth during years of relevant instruction.

3. Groups with more training average better than groups with less.

4. High scoring students can more often solve problems requiring the knowledge than low scoring students.

5. Relationships among items should correspond (show patterns) to relationships among content categories (e.g., results of factor analyses should be logical).

1. Scores for objectives exhibit sensitivity to instruction; i.e., change from wrong to right after effective instruction.

2. Items for one objective are more closely related than across objectives.

3. General background plays less role than in norm-referenced tests (this implies less cultural bias).

4. High scoring students can more often solve problems requiring the knowledge than low scoring students.

5. Relationships among items should correspond (show patterns) to relationships among content categories (e.g., results of factor analyses should be logical).

6. Where a learning hierarchy is known to exist, performance on higher objectives will predict performance on lower order objectives, and demonstrated mastery of lower order objectives facilitates learning of higher order objectives (e.g., positive vertical transfer).

Criterion Related Validity

1. Scores correlate well with other measures of achievement such as teachers' marks and other tests.

2. Scores predict performance in class or on tasks dependent on capabilities being measured.

1. Scores correlate well with other measures of the objective.

Uses

Norm-Referenced Tests (con't.)

1. Assessment of status of school systems (or classes or students) with respect to achievement in basic skills and content areas.

2. Program evaluation for outcomes of long-term growth (at least six months) towards major goals.

3. Selection and placement of students in courses and programs on the basis of level of basic skills or general knowledge of content.

4. Information for curriculum planning.

5. Monitoring yearly progress of schools and school systems with respect to goals.

Criterion-Referenced Tests (con't.)

1. Assessment of status of students (or classes or school system) with respect to curriculum objectives.

2. Program evaluation for long- or short-term attainment of specific objectives.

3. Diagnosis of instructional needs of individual students and groups of students.

4. Information for planning of classroom instruction.

5. Monitoring progress of students with respect to instructional objectives.

From *The Nature and Uses of Criterion-Referenced and Norm-Referenced Achievement Tests: Special Report.* (Vol. 4, No. 3) Burlingame, CA: Association of California School Administrators, n.d.

REFERENCES

Berk, R. A., ed. *Criterion Referenced Measurement: The State of the Art.* Baltimore, MD: The Johns Hopkins University Press, 1980.

Cronbach, L. J. *Essentials of Psychological Testing* (3rd Ed.). New York, NY: Harper & Row, 1970.

Ebel, R. L. *Essentials of Educational Measurement.* Englewood Cliffs, NY: Prentice-Hall, 1972.

Glaser, R. and Nitko, A. J. "Measurement in Learning and Instruction." *Educational Measurement* (2nd Ed.). Edited by R. L. Thorndike. Washington, D.C.: American Council on Education, 1971.

Hambleton, R. K., Swiminathan, H., Algina, J., and Coulson, D. B. "Criterion-Referenced Testing and Measurement: A Review of Technical Issues and Developments," *Review of Educational Research,* 48, 1, (Winter 1978), pp. 1-47.

Harsh, J. R. "The Forest, Trees, Branches, and Leaves Revisited—Norm, Domain, Objective and Criterion-Referenced Assessments for Educational Assessment and Evaluation." Monograph No. 1. Fullerton, CA: Association for Measurement and Evaluation in Guidance, California Personnel and Guidance Association, February 1974.

Mehrens, W. A. and Lehmann, I. J. *Standardized Tests in Education.* (2nd Ed.) New York, NY: Holt, Rinehart & Winston, 1975.

Popham, J. W. *Educational Evaluation.* Englewood Cliffs, NJ: Prentice-Hall, 1975.

Popham, J. W. *Criterion-Referenced Measurement.* New Jersey: Prentice-Hall, 1978.

Research and Evaluation Committee ACSA. *Special Report: The Nature and Uses of Criterion-Referenced and Norm-Referenced Achievement Tests.* Burlingame, CA: Association of California School Administrators, 4, 3, n.d.

Sax, G. "The Use of Standardized Tests in Evaluation." In J. W. Popham (Ed.), *Evaluation in Education: Current Applications.* Berkeley, CA: McCutchan, 1974.

Shoemaker, D. M. "A Framework for Achievement Testing," *Review of Educational Research,* 45, 1 (Winter 1975), pp. 127-147.

UNIT VII

DATA ANALYSIS

	Page
STATISTICS	191
CORRELATION.	197
ANALYSIS OF VARIANCE	205
ITEM RESPONSE THEORY: RASCH MODEL FOR TESTING CALIBRATIONS.	209
CROSS TABULATION	213
STATISTICAL PACKAGES	219

STATISTICS

Statistics is basic to evaluation, and a thorough understanding of the purpose, approach, and method of statistics is a prerequisite for evaluators. The conceptual grasp of statistics is different from learning statistical formulas and possibly even computer operations. That part can be left to the statisticians. The evaluator, however, must know what his data means, and importantly, how to communicate the interpretation of the statistical computations to various audiences.

Statistics is a valuable and powerful tool available to the evaluator, not for his manipulation, but, rather, for his use.

A. DEFINITION, PURPOSE, TYPES

One definition of statistics (Kerlinger, 1973) is "the theory and method of analyzing quantitative data obtained from samples of observations in order to study and compare sources of variance of the phenomena, to help make decisions to accept or reject hypothesized relations between the phenomena, and to aid in making reliable inferences from empirical observations."

1. There are several *purposes* for statistics.

    a. To reduce data to make it more manageable and understandable.

    b. To make thinking about programs definite and exact.

    c. An aid in the study of populations and samples by extracting conclusions drawn from the data.

    d. An aid to decision making.

    e. To allow for prediction of how programs or students will react to a given situation.

    f. For analyzing some possible causal factors that may otherwise remain undiscovered or bewildering.

2. There are *two basic kinds* of statistics.

    a. *Descriptive statistics* aim at summarizing raw data systematically to make it more comprehensible.

    b. *Inferential statistics* are concerned with using data to draw conclusions from a sample about research questions or hypotheses.

B. DESCRIPTIVE STATISTICS

1. Descriptive statistics are *displayed* in a number of ways (see Table 1).

    a. *Frequency tables* display the number of scores that occur within specified frequencies.

    b. Frequency *histograms*—which are very popularly used—represent numbers by rectangles the height of which equal the number of scores at a given interval.

    c. *Frequency polygons* simply connect the midpoints of the tops of each rectangle in a histogram.

    d. *Frequency curves* plot scores on a graph and connect them in a smooth line, and tend to become "bell shaped" with a large number of cases.

    e. A *cumulative frequency curve* is the frequency curve expressed in the terms of the percentage of cases within each score interval.

2. The score around which data tend to center is expressed as a measure of *central tendency*.

    a. The *mean* is the arithmetic average of the scores.

    b. The *median* is the midpoint for all the scores; half the scores fall above the median and half below.

    c. The *mode* is the score that occurs most frequently.

3. *Dispersion* is the term used to describe how spread out the scores are.

    a. The *range* is the difference between the highest and lowest scores.

    b. *Variance*—more complex and difficult to describe—describes the extent to which scores differ from each other; it is an average of the squared deviations (how far each score is away from the mean).

    c. The *standard deviation*—most commonly used description of the spread of scores—is the positive square root of the variance.

C. CHARACTERISTICS OF INFERENTIAL STATISTICS

1. *Statistical significance* is a way of describing the chances that an event will not occur (e.g., an event is studied and has statistical significance at the .05 level, it can then be concluded that if the event were identi-

cally repeated 100 times, the event would occur by chance alone only five times).

2. *Statistical analysis*—necessary in many evaluations—can involve a myriad of statistical procedures, two of the most commonly used of which follow.

   a. The *t-test* is used principally to test hypotheses between two populations (e.g., an evaluator wishes to know if there are statistically significant differences between two groups of trainees on a specified program).

   b. The *F test* (an extension of the t-test) can be used when there are more than two independent random samples of a given normally distributed population (e.g., comparing three methods of reading instruction with students of differing ability levels). See ANALYSIS OF VARIANCE.

D. NONPARAMETRIC STATISTICAL TESTS

Nonparametric statistical tests have many of the same characteristics of parametric statistical tests, but they do not specify conditions about the parameters of the populations from which the samples were drawn. Thus, they may sometimes be used in situations where data will not support other statistical techniques; however, they can lack "power" in the confidence placed in the findings.

Example: A product researcher from a large food company wishes to determine which of three varieties of tomato sauce is the most popular in America. It is impossible to be in every grocery store and count sales, and, almost certainly, brands will sell at different rates in various parts of the country. Since no store can be truly representative of such diversity, inferences based upon a sample may be suspect. Thus, the usual statistical tests cannot be applied with confidence. Nonparametric statistics may be appropriately used. (In this example, the chi square test would be appropriate.)

1. *Advantages* of nonparametric statistical tests.

   a. Probability statements are *exact* probabilities regardless of "normality" of the population from which the sample was drawn.

   b. In small samples (about N=6) nonparametric tests are often required unless the population distribution is known exactly.

   c. Some nonparametric tests can handle samples made up of observations from several different populations.

   d. Some nonparametric statistical tests can treat data in ranks (e.g., a researcher may be able to claim that one subject has more or less of a characteristic without saying how much more or less).

Table 1
Displays for Descriptive Statistics
Frequency Table

Score Interval	Frequency
60 – 64	1
55 – 59	2
50 – 54	3
45 – 49	2
40 – 44	1

Frequency Histogram

Frequency Polygon

Frequency Curve

"Bell-shaped" Curve

Cumulative Frequency Curve

e. Nonparametric tests can treat data which are simply classificatory (e.g., nominal level or measurement).

f. Nonparametric tests are usually much easier to learn and apply than parametric tests.

2. *Disadvantages* of nonparametric statistical tests.

a. If all the assumptions of parametric statistical tests are met, then nonparametric tests are wasteful of data.

b. No nonparametric method presently developed for testing inter-actions in the analysis of variance model.

REFERENCES

Edwards, A. *Statistical Analysis* (3rd Ed.). New York, NY: Holt, 1969.

Guilford, J. P. and Fruchter, B. *Fundamental Statistics in Psychology and Education.* New York, NY: McGraw-Hill, 1973.

Kerlinger, F. N. *Foundations of Behavioral Research* (2nd Ed.). New York, NY: Holt, 1973.

McNemar, Q. *Psychological Statistics* (4th Ed.). New York, NY: Wiley, 1969.

Siegel, S. *Nonparametric Statistics for the Behavioral Sciences.* New York, NY: McGraw-Hill, 1956.

Winer, B. J. *Statistical Principles in Experimental Design* (2nd Ed.). New York, NY: McGraw-Hill, 1971.

CORRELATION

In measurement within the behavioral sciences, a description of the relationship between variables is expressed as a *correlation*. The correlation between variables may denote the existence of an association, or it may give an indication of the degree to which two variables are involved. Correlations do not, by themselves, indicate a causal relationship between variables; however, they can suggest hypotheses about causal relationships. These hypotheses may be tested in scientific investigations to make valid inferences about the suggested causal relationships.

The measurement of the extent to which two variables are related is called the *coefficient of correlation*. Few statistical procedures have opened so many new doors for inquiry within the behavioral sciences as that of correlation.

A. CORRELATION COEFFICIENT

Caution is advised in interpreting correlation and coefficients. While correlation coefficients range from +1 to -1, their size does not represent any absolute fact; rather, correlation coefficients are relative to the situation under which they are derived. In addition to computing coefficients by formulas, correlations are often represented pictorially in scatter diagrams.

1. The greater (or less) the *variability* in measurements, the higher (or lower) will be the correlation coefficient.

    Example: In correlating IQ and GPA for high school students, there may be an r (coefficient of correlation) of +.50, whereas a correlation restricted to just students in graduate school will produce a much lower coefficient.

Example: Five subjects are ranked from first to last on five characteristics: weight, height, math aptitude, running speed, and age. The Spearman rank correlation coefficient would indicate whether or not subjects' rankings on any of these characteristics is directly or inversely related to their rankings on any other characteristic, and also, the strength of that relationship.

1. Has the standard symbol p (called rho).

2. Computationally, an easy technique.

3. A convenient correlational technique when the numbers of pairs is 30 or less (see Kendall's Tau below).

4. While the correlation coefficient is a summary statistic, Spearman allows easy access for examination of individual data.

5. A nonparametric statistical procedure (see STATISTICS); that is, there are no assumptions (with some important limitations and a few exceptions) related to the sample being drawn from a normally distributed population.

6. Formula requires that data be at least of ordinal level of measurement.

7. Should be avoided when interested in the correlation of more than two measures simultaneously.

8. Should be avoided when there are several tied ranks in the data.

9. Caveat: were rankings assigned to the data appropriately (e.g., vital information is lost by starting with continuous data, then rounding the data, and then rank ordering the data)?

D. SPECIALIZED CORRELATION COEFFICIENTS

There are several specialized and less commonly used correlational coefficients. Nearly all (except Kendall's Tau) employ the same product-moment rationale of Pearson.

1. The *tetrachoric correlation coefficient* is used when data for both of the two variables have been artificially reduced to two categories.

   Example: An evaluator wishes to determine the relationship between responses to two questions, and the questions' answers are dichotomized into YES or NO categories regardless of the fact that respondents answered with differing degrees of vigor to the positive or negative side of each question.

   a. Under appropriate conditions, produces a number equivalent to Pearson's r.

   b. Requires that both variables are continuous, linear, and normally distributed.

   c. More difficult than Pearson's r to compute.

    d. More variable, and therefore, less reliable than Pearson's *r*.

2. The *biserial coefficient of correlation* is used when one of two continuous variables is artificially reduced to two categories.

    Example: An evaluator wishes to determine the relationship between scores on a test and students who either passed or failed a driver's training course.

    a. Requires that both variables are linear, and from normally distributed populations (although sample distribution may be skewed).

    b. Designed to be an approximation for Pearson's *r*.

    c. The correlation coefficient can exceed 1 with bimodal or other nonnormal distribution.

    d. Less reliable than Pearson's *r* (standard error is greater), and therefore is the less preferred of the two techniques.

    e. Commonly used technique in test item analysis.

3. The *point biserial correlation coefficient* is used when one of two variables is genuinely dichotomized.

    Example: An evaluator wishes to know the relationship between scores on a test and students who are categorized as male and female.

    a. Produces a lower correlation coefficient than both Pearson's *r* and biserial *r*.

    b. Can be considered as an approximation of Pearson's *r*.

4. The *Phi coefficient of correlation* is used when two correlated distributions are genuinely dichotomized.

    Example: A social scientist wishes to discover the relationship between sex and house ownership versus not owning one.

    a. Closely related to Chi square.

    b. Can be used to determine test-item intercorrelations on multiple choice or two-choice item tests.

    c. Formula is a variation for Pearson's *r*.

5. The *G index of agreement* is a correlational technique which indicates the degree of agreement on a 2 x 2 contingency table.

    a. Based on proportion of agreeing cases as compared with the proportion of disagreeing cases.

    b. A variation of phi coefficient.

    c. Phi and G are not equal and can be far apart.

    d. Advantage is that it does not require any assumptions be made regarding the data.

e. A recently developed statistical technique.

6. *Kendall's Tau* attempts to utilize measurement of the relationship between variables other than the product-moment principle employed by Pearson.

a. Requires both variables to be in rank order.

b. Closely related to Spearman's rho and preferred to it for most inferential statistics.

c. Used often in cases of small N, particularly if N is less than 10, and most especially if N is between 4 and 10.

d. Slightly more difficult to compute than Spearman's rho.

Table 2
Correlational Techniques For Different Forms Of Variables[1]

Technique	Symbol	Variable 1	Variable 2	Remarks
Product-moment correlation	r	Continuous	Continuous	The most stable technique.
Rank-difference correlation (Rho)	p	Ranks	Ranks	Often used instead of product-moment when number of cases is under 30.
Kendall's Tau	τ	Ranks	Ranks	Preferable to Rho for numbers under 10.
Biserial correlation	r_{bis}	Artificial dichotomy	Continuous	Sometimes exceeds 1 — has a larger standard error than r — commonly used in item analysis.
Widespread biserial correlation	r_{wbis}	Widespread artificial dichotomy	Continuous	Used when you are especially interested in persons at the extremes on the dichotomized variable.
Point-biserial correlation	r_{pbis}	True dichotomy	Continuous	Yields a lower correlation than r and much lower than r_{bis}.
Tetrachoric correlation	r_t	Artificial dichotomy	Artificial dichotomy	Used when both variables can be split at critical points.
Phi coefficient	ϕ	True dichotomy	True dichotomy	Used in calculating interitem correlations on multiple choice or two choice items.
Contingency coefficient	C	2 or more categories	2 or more categories	Comparable to r_t under certain conditions — closely related to chi-square.

[1] From Walter R. Borg, *Educational Research: An Introduction.* New York: McKay, 1963.

E. Special cases of correlation rapidly become complex and technically difficult. Although the following outlines are vastly oversimplified, they are presented to acquaint the reader with the existence of some specialized correlational techniques on an awareness level only.

1. A *partial correlation* between two variables occurs when one variable nullifies the effects of a third (or more) variable.

    Example: The correlation coefficient obtained between height and weight of subjects for various ages would be higher than the correlation coefficient obtained at one age level. Age, then, nullifies (or enhances) the strength of the correlation.

    a. A *first order partial correlation* is determined when only one variable is held constant.

    b. A *second order partial correlation* is obtained when two variables are held constant.

2. The *coefficient of multiple correlation* is determined when one wishes to learn the relationship between one variable and two or more others combined with optimal weights.

    Example: A college recruiter wishes to learn the relationship between college freshman GPA and several determinates for academic success, such as high school GPA, achievement test scores, vocational interests, etc.

    a. The theory and techniques of multiple correlation and prediction are complex.

    b. Variables are identified as a *dependent* variable and two or more *independent* variables.

    c. The complexity of multiple correlation and prediction more closely reflect real-world situations.

3. The *correlational ratio* is used for determining the relationship between variables with curvilinear regression.

    Example: A school counselor wishes to determine the relationship between age and scores on a career interest inventory (which tend toward "prestige" careers at one age level and are more widely distributed at other age levels).

    a. Two correlational ratios (called *eta coefficients*) are determined: correlation ratios for the regression of the first variable on the second, and the same for the second variable on the first.

REFERENCES

Anderson, S. B., Ball, S., and Murphy, R. T. *Encyclopedia of Educational Evaluation.* San Francisco, CA: Jossey-Bass, 1975.

Borg, W. R. *Educational Research: An Introduction.* New York, NY: McKay, 1963.

Fisher, R. A. *Statistical Methods for Research Workers.* New York, NY: Hafner, 1958.

Glass, G. V., and Stanley, J. C. *Statistical Methods in Education and Psychology.* New Jersey: Prentice-Hall, 1970.

Guilford, J. P., and Fruchter, B. *Fundamental Statistics in Psychology and Education* (5th Ed.). New York, NY: McGraw-Hill, 1973.

Linert, G. A. "Note on Tests Concerning the G Index of Agreement," *Educational and Psychological Measurement,* 32 (Fall 1972), 281–288.

Maxwell, A. E. "Correlational Techniques." In H. J. Eysenk, W. Arnold, and R. Meili (Eds.), *Encyclopedia of Psychology,* Vol. 1. New York, NY: Herder and Herder, 1972, pp. 221–224.

McNemar, Q. *Psychological Statistics* (4th Ed.). New York, NY: Wiley, 1969.

Siegel, S. *Nonparametric Statistics for the Behavioral Sciences.* New York, NY: McGraw-Hill, 1956.

Thorndike, R. L. and Hagen, E. *Measurement and Evaluation in Psychology and Education* (3rd Ed.). New York, NY: Wiley, 1969.

ANALYSIS OF VARIANCE

The purpose of analysis of variance (ANOVA) is understood more quickly if it is thought of as an extension of the t-test. The t-test is concerned with the equality of two means; i.e., the possible difference between two groups represented by their means on one variable at a time. More than two samples or groups require comparisons between all groups through separate pairings.

Such a procedure can become quite lengthy when there are numerous samples or groups to be compared. In addition to the nearly prohibitive number of calculations, there is another important limitation—the failure to recognize that these samples exist in a set whose elements interact. ANOVA is a sophisticated approach resting upon a series of assumptions and mathematical manipulations. The following outline is designed merely to give the reader an introduction to ANOVA and no pretense is intended that this treatment is thorough enough to enable one to be fully aware of this technique.

Example 1: We have IQ scores on five sample groups of adults. The mean and variance of each group are:

	A	B	C	D	E
Mean	102	123	100	108	121
Variance	15	12	12	14	10

A. BASIC PURPOSE OF ANOVA

1. The question raised by ANOVA is whether the group means differ from one another ("between groups variance") to a greater extent than the scores within each group differ from their own group means ("within groups variance")

   a. "Between groups variance": variation of group means from the total or grand mean of all groups.

b. "Within groups variance": average variability of the scores within each of the groups.

2. If the variation of the group means from the grand mean is greater enough than the variation of the individual scores from their sample means, one may conclude that the groups are different enough to reject a null hypothesis.

3. However, if the between/among groups variance is not substantially greater than the within groups variance, one may conclude that the groups are random samples from the same population.

B. THE F-TEST

1. The F is a ratio of the "between groups variance" and the "within groups variance."

2. Three required conditions for the F-test are:

   a. Groups come from normally distributed populations.

   b. Groups are independent.

   c. Groups possess homogeneity of variance.

Example 2: The SUMMARY TABLE presented below depicts figures drawn from an example in which three *methods* of instruction are used to teach three randomized *groups* of children. A test is given after the instruction and is used as the *criterion.* Group sizes are as follows: Groups I, N = 4; Group II, N = 5; Group III, N = 6.

ANALYSIS OF VARIANCE SUMMARY TABLE

Source of Variation	Sums of Squares	df	Mean Square	F	Significance
Between Groups	15	2	7.50	3.10	N.S.
Within Groups	29	12	2.42		
Total	44	14			

C. EXPLANATION OF SUMMARY TABLE

1. Degrees of Freedom

   a. Between groups df = number of groups minus 1 (3-1) = 2

   b. Within groups df = number within each group minus 1, and then all such df are summed: (4-1) + (5-1) + (6-1) = 12

   c. Total df = 12 + 2 = 14

2. Mean Square

    a. The mean square is also known as the average of the sum of squares divided by its df:

$$\frac{15}{2} = 7.50 \qquad\qquad \frac{29}{12} = 2.42$$

3. The F Statistic

    a. The F statistic is calculated by dividing the between groups mean by the within groups mean square:

$$F = \frac{\text{Mean square for ``between groups''}}{\text{Mean square for ``within groups''}} = \frac{7.50}{2.42} = 3.10$$

4. The calculated F value, 3.10, is compared to the tabled values of F.

    a. If the calculated value is less than the tabled value, the F is not significant.

    b. The null hypothesis—that the differences among the means could have happened by chance (Mean I = Mean II = Mean III)—is not rejected.

    c. The experimental inference is that the methods of instruction are not different in their effect on the criterion (test).

5. The above example is known as "one-way analysis of variance," since there is but one treatment variable (method of instruction).

D. TYPES OF ANOVA

1. One-way analysis of variance has only one treatment variable.

2. Two-way (or three-way) analysis of variance has two (or three, etc.) treatment variables.

3. Multivariate analysis of variance not only has one or more treatment variables, but two or more criterion variables that are analyzed simultaneously.

Type	Independent Variable	Dependent Variable
ANOVA	1 or more	1
MANOVA	1 or more	2 or more

E. NATURE OF VARIABLES

1. Simple analysis of variance must have a *single dependent* variable, also called a criterion variable.

    a. This *dependent* variable must be measured on an *interval* scale.

2. The independent variables can be all nonmetric (categories) or combinations of nonmetric and metric variables.

   a. If a metric variable is used to categorize, it is called and treated as an independent, nonmetric variable.

   b. In ANOVA, the nonmetric independent variables are called *factors.*

3. Hence, one-way analysis of variance investigates the possible effects of a *single independent* variable (factor) on the criterion variable.

   a. If one is interested in the *simultaneous* effects of *n* factors on a single dependent variable, the analysis is referred to as *n*-way analysis of variance.

4. If one is only interested in the effects of *metric* independent variables, the problem is basically that of *multiple regression.*

5. If the user is interested in the effects of both *nonmetric* and *metric* variables, the analysis is referred to as analysis of covariance (ANCOVA).

   a. Here, the nonmetric, independent variables are usually called *factors.*

   b. The metric independent variables are called *covariates.*

F. DISADVANTAGES OF ANOVA

1. Difficult to calculate without the aid of a computer—a must for large populations.

2. Does not reveal the strength of the relation between variables.

3. Becomes distorted (or even inappropriate) by a small sample, particularly when the N's for groups are unequal.

REFERENCES

Guilford, J. P. and Fruchter, B. *Fundamental Statistics in Psychology and Education.* New York, NY: McGraw-Hill, 1973.

Iversen, G. R. and Norpoth, H. *Analysis of Variance.* Beverly Hills, CA: Sage Publications, 1976.

Kerlinger, F. N. *Fundamentals of Behavioral Research* (2nd Ed.). New York, NY: Holt, 1973.

Winer, B. J. *Statistical Principles in Experimental Design* (2nd Ed.). New York, NY: McGraw-Hill, 1971.

ITEM RESPONSE THEORY: RASCH MODEL FOR TESTING CALIBRATIONS

Item response theory is a veiwpoint applicable to test development. The theory of latent traits supposes that individuals have underlying or "hidden" characteristics that cannot be observed directly but may be inferred by an examinee's test score. The latent trait model specifies this relationship. Three principal criteria for latent trait assessment are: (1) the more able a person the better the chance for success on any particular test item; (2) any person has a better chance of correctly answering an easy item than a difficult one; and, (3) these conditions must be observably true regardless of any person's race, sex, or other noninterfering characteristic.

These assumptions differ from traditional test development methodology in that a student's ability is independent of the test items administered to him; and the difficulty of any item is known and calibrated independently of a student or group of students. The Rasch model for test construction and person measurement is the most widely used application of latent trait theory.

The statistical procedures upon which the Rasch model depend are complex. Also, the Rasch model makes some assumptions that not all statisticians and test developers believe are fully valid. Nonetheless, with these cautions, the Rasch model presents evaluators with a flexible and exciting method of dealing with such persistent testing problems as relevance of the test to the curriculum, out-of-level testing of students, equating students' performance on different levels of tests, and test security.

Example: A large, urban school district with students of widely differing abilities, wishes to determine individual student progress as well as make interdistrict comparisons in reading and mathematics. A bank of curriculum test items has been established. With Rasch calibrations, and using the test items in the item bank, various combinations of tests, each for a specified purpose, can easily be constructed and comparisons among these tests can be made.

A. **FUNDAMENTAL ASSUMPTIONS OF THE RASCH MODEL**

1. Any school ability (e.g., reading, mathematics, etc.) can be measured on an *equal interval scale*. Rasch looks beyond a student's score on a particular test to his "true" ability in the subject, regardless of the test used to measure it.

2. Whether or not a student answers a particular item correctly depends upon both the student's achievement in the subject area tested and the difficulty of the test item (e.g., we expect the more able students to have difficulty only with the hardest items, and, conversely, the less able students will probably do well only on the easiest items).

B. **GENERAL CHARACTERISTICS OF THE RASCH MODEL**

1. Items are derived from curriculum specialists and independently calibrated to the measurement scale.

2. Raw scores converted to the underlying scale can then be averaged by class, school, or district.

3. In analyzing test data with the Rasch model, since all forms of a test are drawn from the same calibrated item bank, they are automatically tied to the same underlying measurement scale.

4. When coupled with items from a content-referenced item bank, Rasch is applicable to the development of many kinds of tests, such as competency based assessment, criterion-referenced tests, as well as general survey tests.

5. With conventional testing, the same raw score can represent vastly different levels of student performance, depending upon the length of the test; with Rasch calibrations, however, a raw score is constant from test to test.

6. Reliability is not based on correlation between student scores (as in traditional testing methods), but derived directly from the standard error of measurement for each student.

7. Based upon the reliability information, matches between tests and students can be made.

8. In determining the appropriateness of a particular item, the Rasch model approaches item quality on the *goodness of fit* idea rather than the traditional item discrimination index correlating performance on an item and performance on the test. (See CORRELATION, point biserial.)

9. Rasch methods have been known several years, but are just beginning to be employed practically.

C. GENERAL ADVANTAGES OF THE RASCH MODEL OVER TRADI-TIONAL TEST CALIBRATION METHODS

1. It is possible with Rasch to determine characteristics of a new test even before it is tried out with students.

2. Rasch calibrations can be used even when student abilities are not normally distributed.

3. Item calibrations make it possible to check the scope of the items in the content-referenced item bank to be sure that all achievement levels are covered.

4. Rasch presents a strong, flexible basis for comparing student achievement across tests.

5. The scale permits test developers to determine which items would be appropriate to include for any particular test level.

6. The scale allows test developers to avoid asking a student to answer items that are obviously too hard for him, or are ridiculously easy.

7. Rasch calibrations permit comparisons of student achievement longitudinally (from year to year) even though a student will take different levels of the tests.

8. By selecting only items which directly reflect a specific curricular goal, the scale aids in developing criterion-referenced tests.

9. The model enhances the updating of tests by field testing a few new items each time, and thus eliminating the need for renorming.

10. Because as many parallel forms of the test can be developed as is desired, test security is enhanced.

D. SCHOOL DISTRICT NEEDS IMPLICIT IN RASCH METHODOLOGY (Adapted from "Everything You Wanted to Know About the Rasch.")

1. The need to directly relate student progress to the curriculum in which he is instructed rather than to an external reference group.

2. The need to determine a student's progress longitudinally as he moves through the curriculum (from year to year) and his ability level changes.

3. The need to develop parallel test forms for students at differing ability levels which are truly comparable of measuring student performance.

4. The need to develop comparability between norm-referenced tests and criterion-referenced tests.

5. The need to report to teachers student progress in terms of overall achievement as well as in terms of achievement on specific learning goals or objectives.

6. The need to more accurately specify item difficulty without over-testing one group of students.

7. The need to develop parallel test forms to insure test security.

REFERENCES

Foster, F. "Everything You Wanted to Know About Rasch." Portland, OR: Portland Public Schools, 1977.

Hambleton, R. K., Swaminathan, H., Cook, L. L., Eignor, D. R., & Gifford, J. A. "Developments in Latent Trait Theory: Models, Technical Issues, and Applications," *Review of Educational Research,* 48 (Fall, 1978), pp. 467-510.

Rentz, R. R. & Rentz, C. C. *Does the Rasch Model Really Work? A Discussion for Practitioners.* ERIC Report No. 67. Princeton, N. J.: ERIC Clearinghouse on Tests, Measurement, and Evaluation, Educational Testing Service, 1978.

Warm, T. A. *A Primer of Item Response Theory.* U.S. Coast Guard Institute. Oklahoma City, OK, December, 1978.

Wright, B. D. & Stone, M. H. *Best Test Design.* Chicago, MESA Press, 1979.

CROSS TABULATION

After he examines the distribution of the variables under consideration, the researcher normally begins to investigate potential relationships between sets of two or more of these variables. If he has access to the many pre-packaged statistical programs, the investigator may choose to do contingency table (cross tabulation) analysis, correlation analysis, regression analysis, or analysis of variance. The procedure that he chooses will depend upon the characteristics of the variables: their level of measurement, whether they are discrete or continuous, as well as the general research design.

In this unit, a close examination is made of cross tabulation analysis, one of the more commonly used approaches to data analysis in the behavioral sciences. Basically, cross tabulation allows the researcher to expand the area under investigation through the addition of other classificatory variables such as controls, and through the addition of categories within the variables selected.

A. DEFINITION

1. A cross tabulation (also referred to as *cross break* and *contingency table*) is a joint frequency distribution of cases as defined by the categories of two or more variables.

   a. The display of the distribution of cases is the chief component of contingency table analysis.

   b. Cross tabulation is the most commonly used method of analysis in the social sciences.

   c. Cross tabulation can be used with nearly any kind of data. Entries are usually in the form of frequencies or percentages.

   d. Cross tabulation allows the study and testing of relationships between two variables while controlling for the effects of a third variable—spurious relationships are uncovered.

e. Cross tabulation indicates what goes with what in the research design, thereby exposing misconceptions and/or design inadequacies.

f. Contingency tables are most commonly found in the 2 x 2 design. Other designs include: 2 x 3; 3 x 3; 3 x 4, etc. Tables in excess of 5 x 5 tend to be unclear and difficult to analyze.

B. SUMMARY STATISTICS FOR CROSS TABULATIONS

1. Often it is desirable to summarize the relationship depicted in a cross tabulation table with a measure of association *or* a test of statistical significance.

2. The Chi-square statistic will indicate the likelihood that the variables are statistically independent; i.e., that no relationship exists between the variables as they exist in the universe.

   a. While some small deviations can be reasonably expected due to chance, large deviations (large values of Chi square) are unlikely.

   b. Although the Chi-square statistic itself is not a probability, it can be converted into a probability figure which is customarily called the significance level.

   c. Standard computer programs (such as SPSS: see STATISTICAL PACKAGES) do the above conversion and prints the significance level along with the Chi-square value.

3. When the sample is very large, even slight (miniscule) deviations will generate a statistically significant Chi square.

   a. Larger samples are much more likely to approximate true relationships in the universe.

   b. Small samples are more likely to contain a disproportionate number of atypical cases.

   c. Actually, significance tests are mostly a measure of whether the sample under consideration is sufficiently large to be undisturbed by the chance selection of unrepresentative cases.

   d. The mere fact that a relationship is statistically significant does not mean that the degree of relationship is important in the context of the research being conducted.

   e. The Chi-square statistic does not report the strength of the association.

4. The choice of a test of significance or a measure of association depends in part upon the level of measurement of the variables employed in the cross tabulation (also involved are: linear versus curvilinear association and number of categories—rows and columns, etc.).

a. Chi square, Cramer's V, the Contingency Coefficient, Lambda, and the uncertainty coefficient assume both variables to have been measured at the *nominal level*.

b. At least ordinal-level measurement is required for both variables when the tau b, tau c, gamma, or Somer's D measures of association are being used.

Example 1: CROSS TABULATION: Course Grade X Academic Standing in High School

COUNT ROW PCT COL PCT TOT PCT	ACADEMIC STANDING IN HIGH SCHOOL					
	Top 10%	Top 25%	Top 50%	Lower 50%	Don't Know	Row
Grade	1	2	3	4	5	Total
A 1	17 47.2 31.5 10.4	12 33.3 21.1 7.4	3 8.3 15.0 1.8	1 2.8 20.0 0.6	3 8.3 11.1 1.8	36 22.1
B 2	21 30.9 38.9 12.9	26 38.2 45.6 16.0	5 7.4 25.0 3.1	3 4.4 60.0 1.8	13 19.1 48.1 8.0	68 41.7
C 3	9 26.5 16.7 5.5	13 38.2 22.8 8.0	5 14.7 25.0 3.1	1 2.9 20.0 0.6	6 17.6 22.2 3.7	34 20.9
D 4	1 33.3 1.9 0.6	0 0.0 0.0 0.0	1 33.3 5.0 0.6	0 0.0 0.0 0.0	1 33.3 3.7 0.6	3 1.8
F 5	0 0.0 0.0 0.0	1 25.0 1.8 0.6	2 50.0 10.0 1.2	0 0.0 0.0 0.0	1 25.0 3.7 0.6	4 2.5
INC 6	4 44.4 7.4 2.5	2 22.2 3.5 1.2	3 33.3 15.0 1.8	0 0.0 0.0 0.0	0 0.0 0.0 0.0	9 5.5
CR 7	2 22.2 3.7 1.2	3 33.3 5.3 1.8	1 11.1 5.0 0.6	0 0.0 0.0 0.0	3 33.3 11.1 1.8	9 5.5
Column	54	57	20	5	27	163
Total	33.1	35.0	12.3	3.1	16.6	100

Example 2: CROSS TABULATION: Income X Race

INCOME	COUNT COL PCT	RACE 1 WHITE	2 NON- WHITE	ROW TOTAL
Less than $4000	1	66 24.6	42 58.3	108 31.8
$4000 – $7999	2	93 34.7	21 29.2	114 33.5
$8000 – $14,999	3	82 30.6	7 9.7	89 26.2
$15,000 and over	4	27 10.1	2 2.8	29 8.5
Column Total		268 78.8	72 21.2	340 100

Chi Square = 33.80762   with 3 Degrees of Freedom
Significance = 0.000

It is evident that there is a strong relationship between race and income. The proportion of Whites in the higher income categories is considerably greater than the proportion of non-Whites in those categories, while the opposite is true in the lower income categories.

Example 3: CROSS TABULATION: Income X Race (Controlling for Education)

   1. Less than High School   2. High School or more

| INCOME | COUNT COL PCT | RACE | | ROW TOTAL |
		WHITE	NON-WHITE	
Less than $41000	1	51	31	82
		42.1	72.1	50.0
$4000 – $7999	2	44	9	53
		36.4	20.9	32.3
$8000 – $14,999	3	26	2	28
		21.5	4.7	17.1
$15,000 and over	4	0	1	1
		0.0	2.3	0.6
Column Total		121	43	164
		73.8	26.2	100

Chi Square = 16.10907
Significance = 0.0011   with 3 Degrees of Freedom

From Example 2, it was evident that a strong relationship exists between race and income. A second hypothesis, that this relationship exists even when controlling for levels of education, requires a three-dimensional table (race x income x education). Because printing surfaces are two-dimensional, three-dimensional tables are usually presented as a series of two-dimensional tables on separate computer printout pages.

The above table includes only those cases with the value indicated above by the numeral 1 on the variable "education;" i.e., those subjects whose schooling was "less than high school."

   c. Note: These statistics may be applied to tables composed of variables measured at a higher level, but the statistics are computed as if the variables were measured at only the nominal level.

   d. Eta assumes that the independent variable is nominal level and the dependent variable is interval level.

   e. When both variables are at the interval or ratio level, the Pearson product-moment correlation is the most appropriate measure of association.

EXAMPLE

Since the above measures of association describe the degree to which the values of one variable *predict* or *vary* with those of another, the following examples of cross tabulation are used to answer questions under investigation.

Example 1:   Can one predict a student's success in a first-year college course on the basis of his academic standing in high school?

Conclusion: Superior high school students did not always excel in this course.

Based on these findings: Only one-third of the students who were in the top 10 percent of their high school classes received an A for the course. Twenty percent of the students who had a B average in high school received an A for the course. (See Example 1.)

REFERENCES

Kerlinger, F. *Foundations of Behavioral Research* (2nd Ed.). New York, NY: Holt, Rinehart and Winston, 1973.

Siegel, S. *Nonparametric Statistics for the Behavioral Sciences.* New York, NY: McGraw-Hill, 1956.

Upton, G. The Analysis of Cross-Tabulated Data. New York, NY: John Wiley & Sons, 1978.

STATISTICAL PACKAGES

The advent of packaged, prewritten statistical programs has reduced the necessity for researchers/evaluators to be highly cognizant of computer programming. These packages offer a variety of frequently used manipulative and statistical procedures which are stored in the computer for future use. Consequently, it is no longer necessary to write a detailed program each time one wants to execute a particular function. Since the directions for executing such programs are quite simple and straightforward, one needs know only a few routines to access these packaged programs.

A. COMMON CHARACTERISTICS OF PREWRITTEN PROGRAMS

1. They have almost identical sets of prewritten procedures.

   a. Users can issue commands to transform data, manipulate files, and calculate various types of statistical analyses.

   b. Likewise, users can modify files, generate new sorts on variables, etc.

2. They have a set of integrated control statements which allows users to access a variety of procedures with basically the same format.

   a. *Keyword* commands activate specific programs; e.g., in SPSS, the keyword FREQUENCIES directs the computer to calculate frequency distributions.

   b. *Specification* commands establish delimiting parameters on keyword commands; e.g., specification itemizes the variables to be cross tabulated.

   c. *Delimiter* commands separate keywords and specifications and items within specifications; e.g., most commonly used delimiters are the BLANK, COMMA, and SLASH.

   d. *Option* commands allow the user to select certain standard manipulative and statistical procedures from the entire package.

3. They utilize a natural-language format.

    a. Programming statements are often written in straightforward every-day English; e.g., an SPSS command to calculate a Pearson's product moment correlation is simply PEARSON CORR.

4. They access data from a variety of sources.

    a. Data cards (either keypunched or direct read).

    b. Magnetic tape or disc.

    c. Hand-fed data directly by the operator.

B. STATISTICAL PACKAGE FOR THE SOCIAL SCIENCES (SPSS)

1. Developed at Stanford, made available in the late 1960s, now housed in the National Opinion Research Center at the University of Chicago.

2. Main objective: to provide a set of manipulative and statistical programs that can be easily handled by computer-naive social scientists.

3. The following programs are included: various descriptive statistics, frequency distributions, cross-tabulation matrices, simple and multiple correlations, scatter diagrams, partial correlations, means and variances for stratified populations, analyses of variance and covariance, simple and multiple regression analysis, discriminant analysis, factor analysis, canonical analysis, and Guttman scaling.

4. SPSS can also generate new variables from a combination of older ones; delete, combine, recode, and collapse existent variables; categorize, select, or weigh specific cases; and add variables to a file.

C   ORGANIZED SET OF INTEGRATED ROUTINES FOR INVESTIGATION WITH STATISTICS (OSIRIS)

1. Developed by the Institute for Social Research at the University of Michigan during the late 1950s.

2. Since the package evolved from survey research conducted by ISR, its primary objective is to provide a combination of procedures for editing data and applying multivariate analyses.

3. OSIRIS has been expanded to include: organization and editing card image data, copying and subsetting data, transforming data values, projecting univariate and bivariate frequency distributions, plotting scatter plots, developing correlational analyses as well as multiple regression analyses and multivariate analyses of variance with nominal, ordinal, or metric variables, factor analyses, multidimensional scaling, and cluster analyses.

4. As in SPSS, each program can be executed separately or in a chain; i.e., the output from one function can be fed as input to another.

D. BIOMEDICAL COMPUTER PROGRAMS (BMD)

1. Developed at the UCLA Medical Center in the early 1960s for medical research, the statistical and mathematical procedures are conveniently adaptable to various types of social research.

2. The stock BMD programs include: description and tabulations, producing various descriptive and bivariate correlations; regression analysis, providing simple and multiple regression coefficients; time-series analysis, generating statistics to examine change-over time; variance analysis, yielding coefficients for analyses of variance and covariance; multivariate analysis, treating mathematical models such as factor analysis, discriminant analysis, and canonical analysis; special programs, providing for Guttman scaling and techniques for transforming data.

3. As with SPSS and OSIRIS, the BMD programs may be run in succession, with each program based on output from preceding analyses.

E. HEWLETT-PACKARD SUPPORTED PROGRAMS (HP)

1. Developed by a private firm, Hewlett-Packard, specifically for HP equipment (HP is a major designer and manufacturer of electronics hardware and software).

2. HP has developed a library of programs all written in BASIC language, an "easy" language for the nonvice to handle.

    a. HP has also developed analogous programs written in FORTRAN, ALGOL, and HP ASSEMBLY language suitable for non-BASIC language systems.

3. User input is organized into three procedures: data definition (entry); data editing; and data display.

4. In addition to probability and statistical packages, HP offers packages for mathematics and numerical analysis, scientific and engineering applications, business and manufacturing applications, and others.

5. It is widely used in public school districts for research and evaluation analyses.

F. SIMILARITIES AND DIFFERENCES

1. All these packages have identical objectives and perform basically the same manipulative and statistical functions.

2. They can only be activated via batch mode.

    a. Although interaction with a program while it is being executed currently is impossible, interactive package programs are being developed.

3. SPSS is probably the easiest to work with since its manual is most readable and explains all the statistical operations available to the user.

4. Each package contains some unique functions.

   a. Only OSIRIS can perform certain types of cluster analyses and multidimensional scaling and utilize multiple response variables.

   b. OSIRIS and BMD can be used with smaller computing systems, with, perhaps, faster turn-around time.

G. STATISTICAL ANALYSIS SYSTEM (SAS)

1. Developed by the SAS Institute, P.O. Box 10066, Raleigh, N.C. 27605 in the late 1960's.

2. SAS has developed a library of programs written in PL1 in support of IBM systems.

3. Provides for more statistical procedures than other packages and allows for program writing.

REFERENCES

Dixon, W. J. (Ed.). *Biomedical Computer Programs.* Berkeley, CA: University of California Press, 1975.

Helwig, J. T. and Council, K. (Eds.) *SAS Users Guide,* 1979 Edition. Raleigh, N.C.: SAS Institute, 1979.

Hewlett-Packard Company. *HP BASIC Program Library Handbook.* Cupertino, CA: Hewlett-Packard Company, 1972.

Institute for Social Research. *OSIRIS III.* Ann Arbor, MI: University of Michigan, 1973.

Nie, N. et al. *Statistical Package for the Social Sciences.* New York, NY: McGraw-Hill, 1975.

White, D. *Statistics for Education: With Data Processing.* New York, NY: Harper and Row, 1973.

UNIT VIII

REPORTING RESULTS

	Page
EXPRESSING TEST RESULTS.	225
EVALUATION REPORTING FORMAT	231

EXPRESSING TEST RESULTS

A test score acquires meaning only when it is compared with an appropriate standard, typically either with the scores of an well-identified group of subjects or against a predetermined criterion. When an individual's test score is expressed in terms of its relative status within a group, it can be reported on several alternative *test scales*. The uses to which the test score will be put determine which test scale is appropriate. The principal benefit of standardized test scales is their ability to transform test scores into common units so that comparisons within tests (an individual's score against others who have taken the same test) and between tests (scores on one test against scores on a different test) can be made.

A. NORMAL CURVE

The normal curve—the common standard to which all test scales relate—denotes the percentage of cases that can be expected to fall within certain ranges when expressed in terms of standard deviation units (see following table).

1. The mean raw score (average number of items correct) for a group is designated by a zero at the center of the baseline of the normal curve.

    Example: If 2000 military recruits obtain an average of 71 items correct on a general classification test, then the score 71 would fall on the zero point for the normal curve; by definition, 50 percent of the cases would fall above this point and 50 percent below (assuming a perfectly normally distributed population).

2. The baseline is divided into standard deviation units.

    Example: If, on the same test as above, ±4 was one standard deviation unit on the recruits' test performance, one could expect the scores for 34 percent of the recruits to fall

CHART COMPARING VARIOUS TEST SCORES AND THEIR CORRESPONDENCE TO EACH OTHER[1]

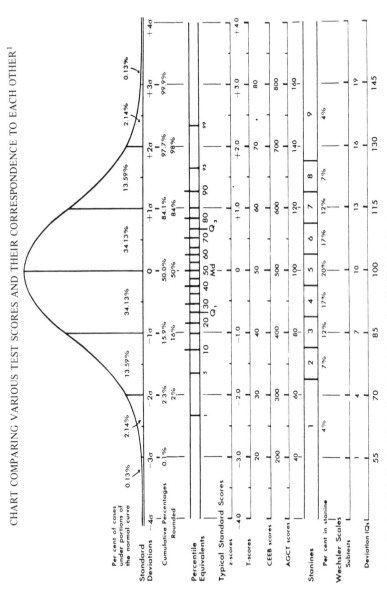

1. Test Service Bulletin Number 48, The Psychological Corporation, 304 East 45th Street, New York, New York 10017.

between 71 and 75 raw score points correct; conversely, one could expect another 34 percent of the recruits to obtain scores between 67 and 71 raw score points correct.

3. Note that while the standard deviation remains constant for all examinees, the percentage of cases one can expect to fall within its limits becomes increasingly smaller with each succceding standard deviation unit away from the mean.

4. Note that nearly all the cases, for any normally distributed population, will fall within ±2 standard deviation units away from the mean score for the group.

METHODS OF EXPRESSING TEST SCORES FIGURE HERE

NOTE: This chart cannot be used to equate scores on one test to scores on another test. For example, both 600 on the CEEB and 120 on the AGCT are one standard deviation above their respective means, but they do not represent "equal" standings because the scores were obtained from different groups.

From *Test Service Bulletin No. 48.* New York: The Psychological Corporation, 1955.

Example: Deviation from the mean	-2	- 1	0	+1	+2
Percentile equivalent	2	16	50	84	98

B. STANDARD SCORES

Standard scores are raw score test conversions to common units, thus allowing comparisons of different tests.

1. *Z scores* are simply the numerical equivalent of standard deviations.

   Example: Using the above recruit example, a raw score of 77 (one and one-half standard' deviation units above the mean) would produce a z score of +1.5.

   a. Can be computed for distributions other than normal.

   b. Usually sufficient to compute to a single decimal place.

   c. Commonly used for gross test score comparisons.

2. *T scores* equate the mean of the raw scores to 50, and have a standard deviation of 10.

   Example: A z score of +1.5 equals a T score of 65.

   a. Directly related to z scores.

   b. Eliminates negative numbers, thus facilitating many computations.

    c. Usually expressed in whole numbers from 20 to 80.

    d. Popularized by Navy use during World War II.

  3. *CEEB scores* arbitrarily set 500 points as the mean and 100 points as one standard deviation unit.

      Example: A college recruiter knows that an applicant with a 550 score on the SAT is .5 standard deviation units above the mean.

    a. Derived by the College Entrance Examination Board.

    b. Eliminates both negative numbers and decimals.

    c. Very popularly used in several college admission tests today.

  4. *AGCT scores* set 100 as the mean and 20 as one standard deviation.

      Example: An army applicant with a recruiting test score of 80 is one standard deviation below the average score on the test.

    a. Derived by Army during World War II for Army General Classification Test.

    b. Merely, two times T scores.

C. **STANINES**

  Stanines (or *standard nines*) divides the general standard score system into nine groups.

  Example: Using the Army recruit example from above, any score of 69 to 73 (±1 standard deviation) would be within the fifth stanine.

  1. Stanine 9 is top and stanine 1 is bottom.

  2. Except for stanine 9 and 1, all spreads are one-half standard deviation units above and below where they normally fall, thus straddling standard deviation ranges.

  3. Resultant stanine distribution has a mean of 5.0 and standard deviation of 2.0.

  4. Percentage of cases within each stanine is defined and usually listed immediately below the stanine scale.

  5. Practically, nine units occupy only one column on computer card-punch records (a major consideration in its development).

  6. Loss of fine discrimination among cases within categories is its major disadvantage, particularly in counseling and guidance work.

  7. Was the standard for the Army Air Force Psychology Program during World War II.

  8. Developed by J. P. Guilford and other psychologists.

D. WECHSLER SCALE

Wechsler scales converts a subject's raw scores on each Wechsler IQ test subtest to a standard score.

1. Requires an appropriate norms table.

2. Based on a mean of 10 and a standard deviation of 3.

3. Wechsler IQ test scores are based on a standard score mean of 100 with a standard deviation of 15 (based on a theoretical "average" IQ range).

4. IQs derived using Wechsler scales are called *deviation IQ,* as contrasted with IQ more conventionally derived from mental age divided by chronological age.

5. Wechsler scale tied exclusively to Wechsler intelligence tests.

6. Used primarily in clinical diagnostic situations.

7. Less popularly used than in previous years.

REFERENCES

Glass, G. V. and Stanley, J. C. *Statistical Methods in Education and Psychology.* New Jersey: Prentice-Hall, 1970.

Guilford, J. P. and Fruchter, B. *Fundamental Statistics in Psychology and Education* (5th Ed.). New York, NY: McGraw-Hill, 1973.

Test Service Bulletin No. 48. New York, NY: The Psychological Corporation, 1955.

EVALUATION REPORTING FORMAT

The reporting format of an evaluation report can be as varied as there are evaluators. The factor which most influences the format is the audience(s) to whom the report is directed. The trend is now toward an executive report which is a shortened form with clearly marked sections and a summary of the important findings and conclusions. The authors suggest a format which is simple and easily followed.

A. REPORTING FORMAT

1. *Introduction:* The introduction should state the purpose of the report, the audience(s) addressed, and reporting periods; i.e., initial, interim, and final. There should be some indication of the materials to be included in each of the reports. If the study has been delimited, these delimitations will be included in this section also.

2. *Areas to be investigated:* Each report (initial, interim, and final) should carry a brief outline of the areas being investigated and reported. This will keep the reader informed as to what the entire study will include and what has or has not been included in the report being considered.

Example:

I. The Influence of Attendance at Selected Program Activities on the Participant's School Life

   1. Attendance at School

      a. Participant's attendance at selected activities as compared to the participant's school attendance records.

      b. Participant's school attendance records as compared to their school's overall attendance records.

2. Grade Point Average

    a.   The effect of participant's GPA after one year in the selec-
ted activities program as compared with his GPA before
entering the program.

    b.   The effect of participant's GPA as compared to the GPA of
a comparison group drawn from the total school population.

3. Disciplinary Referrals at School

    a.   Attendance at selected activities as compared to the num-
ber of disciplinary referrals in which participants were
involved at their respective schools.

4. *Philosophy:* A statement of philosophy of the organization
being evaluated should be included. If there are any comments
about the philosophy, they should be placed after the philosophy, they should be placed after the philosophy statement;
e.g., how it was derived, its inadequateness, etc.

5. *Goals and objectives:* The goals and objectives should be outlined in clear declarative statements. The distinction between
goals and objectives should be made for ease of reading.

6. *Anonymity and confidentiality of data:* The laws concerning
anonymity and confidentiality of data are now very clearly
stated. For the safety of the evaluator, a statement stating that
the data collected will be used in the strictest confidentiality
and will not be shared with a third party should be included.
Data selected for use should be coded, condensed, and reported
without any identification of participants.

    Example: The evaluation team fully appreciates the restric-
tions placed on the report by the recent Buckley
Amendment (Section C, Regulations of the Family
Rights and Privacy Amendment to the 1974 Equal
Education Act); therefore, at no time will comparisons be made between/among individuals, participants, and staff, and/or participating schools. Numbered codification arrangements will be developed
to insure needed anonymity and to guarantee the
confidentiality of school and law enforcement
agency records.

7. *Executive report summary:* The section should include a summary of the major findings, conclusions, and recommendations.
These will assist those individuals who wish to know, but who
do not wish to take the time to read the entire port, or thumb
through, reading only conclusion sections. This section also

assists the administrative staff who contracted the evaluation in making immediate changes, conducting public relations campaigns, involving others, etc.

8. *Evaluation reporting:* The evaluation reporting section should be divided into several sections. The authors agree that the following format is conducive to the ease of reporting, reading, and understanding.

a. *The evaluation statement:* Using the areas to be investigated, an evaluation statement should be developed for each area. This statement should clearly state what is being evaluated. Hypothesis formation is not out of order.

b. *Rationale statement:* A short paragraph indicating the rationale for including and carrying out the investigation is included here. A search of the literature will assist the evaluator in justifying the investigation.

c. *Population sample:* A statement defining the sample population and the sampling technique are to be included here. The statement should be succinct and to the point.

d. *Instrumentation and/or data collection:* Here should be included the source(s) of the data, who will collect these data, and how the data was collected. Description of collection instruments and their development should be included in an appendix. It is not out of place to insert the data collection instrument following the evaluation statement and its data.

e. *Data analysis:* A description of the statistical analysis is placed here. A reporting of the findings and any charts, graphs, or tables are also included. It is this section upon which rests the evaluation report.

f. Conclusion(s): Under this section the evaluator draws a conclusion or conclusions based upon the data reported. Care must be taken to refer only to the data reported.

g. *Recommendation(s)* (optional): Recommendations are based directly upon the data reported and the conclusions drawn. The recommendations should be clearly stated and be implementable by the organization being evaluated.

B. CONSIDERATIONS

1. This format is flexible enough to suit most evaluation reporting. Sections can be added or eliminated to best fit the situation.

2. The contracting agent should approve any evaluation reporting format.

REFERENCES

A Manual of Style (12th Ed.). Chicago, IL: University of Chicago Press, 1969.

American Psychological Association. *Publication Manual of the American Psychological Association* (1967 Revision). Washington, D.C.: American Psychological Association, 1967.

Strunk, W. and White, E. *The Elements of Style.* New York, NY: MacMillan, 1959.

BIBLIOGRAPHY

A Manual of Style (12th Ed.). Chicago, IL: University of Chicago Press, 1969.

Adams, R. N. and Preiss, J. J. (Eds.). *Human Organization Research.* Homewood, IL: Dorsey Press, 1960.

American Psychological Association. *Publication Manual of the American Psychological Association* (1967 Revision). Washington, D.C.: American Psychological Association, 1967.

American Psychological Association. *Standards for Educational and Psychological Tests.* Washington, D.C., 1974.

Anderson, N. H. "Scales and Statistics: Parametric and Nonparametric," *Psychological Bulletin,* 58 (April 1961). 305-16.

Anderson, R. D., Soptick, J. M., Rogers, W. T., & Worthen, B. R. An Analysis and Interpretation of Tasks and Competencies Required of Personnel Conducting Exemplary Research and Research-Related Activities in Education. Technical Paper No. 23. Boulder, CO: AERA Task Force on Research Training, Laboratory of Educational Research, 1971.

Anderson, S. B., Ball, S., and Murphy, R. T. *Encyclopedia of Educational Evaluation.* San Francisco, CA: Jossey-Bass, 1975.

Argyris, C. "Some Unintended Consequences of Rigorous Research." *Psychological Bulletin,* 70 (September 1968), pp. 185-197.

Arnfield, R. V. (Ed.). *Technological Forecasting.* Chicago, IL: Aldine Publishing Company, 1969.

Baker, F. B. "Advances in Item Analysis," *Review of Educational Research,* 47, 1977, pp. 151-178.

Berdie, D. R. and Anderson, J. F. *Questionnaires: Design and Use.* New Jersey: The Scarecrow Press, Inc., 1974.

Berelson, B. *Content Analysis in Communication Research.* Glencoe, IL: Free Press, 1952.

Berk, Ronald A. ed. *Criterion Referenced Measurement: The State of the Art.* Baltimore, MD: The Johns Hopkins University Press, 1980.

Best, J. W. *Research in Education.* Englewood Cliffs, NJ: Prentice-Hall, Inc., 1970.

Borg, W. R. *Educational Research: An Introduction.* New York, NY: David McKay Company, Inc., 1963.

Brown, F. G. *Principles of Educational and Psychological Testing.* New York, NY: Holt, Rinehart and Winston, 1976.

Campbell, D. T. "Reforms as Experiments," *American Psychologist,* 1969, 24, 409-429.

Campbell, D. T. "The Informant in Quantitative Research," *American Journal of Sociology,* 1955, 60, 339-342.

Campbell, D. T. and Stanley, J. C. *Experimental and Quasi-Experimental Designs for Research.* Chicago, IL: Rand McNally, 1963.

Campbell, D. T. and Stanley, J. C. *Experiments and Quasi-Experimental Designs for Research on Teaching.* Chicago, IL: Rand McNally, 1966.

Center for Futures Research. *Annual Report 1976 and Five-Year Review, 1971-76.* Los Angeles, CA: University of Southern California Graduate School of Business Administration, 1976.

Cochran, W. G. *Sampling Techniques,* (2nd Ed.), New York, NY: Wiley, 1963.

Coleman, J. S. "Evaluating Educational Programs: A Symposium," *The Urban Review,* 1969, 3 (4). 6-8.

Collins, A. *The Interview: An Educational Research Tool.* Palo Alto, CA: ERIC/IR, 1970.

Cox, J. *Basics of Questionnaire Construction in Educational Settings.* Los Angeles, CA: Office of the Los Angeles County Superintendent of Schools, 1976.

Cronbach, L. J. *Essentials of Psychological Testing* (3rd Ed.). New York, NY: Harper & Row, 1970.

Dalkey, N. C., et al. *The Delphi Method: An Experimental Study of Group Opinion.* Santa Monica, CA: The Rand Corporation, 1972.

Davis, F. B. *Item Analysis Data.* Cambridge, MA: Harvard University, 1946.

Dillman, D. "Increasing Mail Questionnaire Response in Large Samples of the General Public," *Public Opinion Quarterly,* 36, (Summer 1972) 254-7.

Dixon, W. J. (Ed.). *Biomedical Computer Programs,* Berkeley, CA: University of California Press, 1975.

Downs, A. "Some Thoughts on Giving People Economic Advice," *American Behavioral Scientist,* 1965, 9 (1), 30-32.

Dyer, H. S. *The Interview as a Measuring Device in Education.* Princeton, NJ: ERIC/TM, 1976.

Ebel, R. L. *Essentials of Educational Measurement.* Englewood Cliffs, NY: Prentice-Hall, 1972.

Edwards, A. *Statistical Analysis* (3rd Ed.). New York, NY: Holt, 1969.

English, H. B. and English, A. C. *A Comprehensive Dictionary of Psychological and Psychoanalytical Terms.* New York, NY: David McKay Company, 1958.

ERIC/TM. *Selecting Educational Researchers and Evaluators.* TM Report 48. Princeton: ERIC/TM.

Fincher, C. "Differential Validity and Test Bias," *Personnel Psychology,* 28, 1975, pp. 481-500.

Fisher, R. *The Design of Experiments.* (6th Ed.), New York, NY: Hafner 1951.

Fisher, R. A. *Statistical Methods for Research Workers.* New York, NY: Hafner, 1958.

Flanders, N. A. *Interaction Analysis in the Classroom: A Manual for Observers.* Ann Arbor, MI: School of Education, University of Michigan, 1966.

Foster, F. "Everything You Wanted to Know About Rasch." Portland, OR: Portland Public Schools, 1977.

Fox, D. J. *The Research Process in Education.* New York, NY: Holt, Rinehart and Winston, 1969.

Fox, R. S., Schmuck, R., Van Egmond, E., Ritvo, M., and Jung, C. *Diagnosing Professional Climate of Schools.* NTL Learning Resources Corporation, Inc., Fairfax, VA, 1973.

Freeman, H. E. and Sherwood, C. "Research in Large Scale Intervention Programs," *Journal of Social Issues,* 1965, 21, 11-28.

Gardner, P. L. "Scales and Statistics," *Review of Educational Research,* 45 (Winter, 1975), 43-57.

Gephart, W. J. and Antonoplos, D. P. "The Effects of Expectancy and Other Research-Biasing Factors." *Phi Delta Kappan,* 50 (June 1969), pp. 579-583.

Glaser, R. and Nitko, A. J. "Measurement in Learning and Instruction." *Educational Measurement* (2nd Ed.). Edited by R. L. Thorndike. Washington, D.C.: American Council on Education, 1971.

Glass, G. V., and Stanley, J. C. *Statistical Methods in Education and Psychology.* New Jersey: Prentice-Hall, 1970.

Gorden, R. L. *Interviewing: Strategy, Techniques, and Tactics* (Rev. Ed.). Homewood, IL: The Dorsey Press, 1975.

Greenberg, B. G. "Evaluation of Social Programs," *Review of the International Statistical Institute,* 1968, 36, 260-277.

Guilford, J. P. *Psychometric Methods.* New York, NY: McGraw-Hill, 1954.

Guilford, J. P., and Fruchter, B. *Fundamental Statistics in Psychology and Education* (5th Ed.). New York, NY: McGraw-Hill, 1973.

Hambleton, R. K., Swiminathan, H., Algina, J., and Coulson, D. B. "Criterion-Referenced Testing and Measurement: A Review of Technical Issues and Developments," *Review of Educational Research,* 48, 1, (Winter 1978), pp. 1-47.

Hambleton, R. K., Swaminathan, H., Cook, L. L., Eignor, D. R., & Gifford, J. A. "Developments in Latent Trait Theory: Models, Technical Issues, and Applications," *Review of Educational Research,* 48 (Fall, 1978), pp. 467-510.

Hammond, P. E. (Ed.). *Sociologists at Work.* New York, NY: Basic Books, 1964.

Harman, H. H. *Modern Factor Analysis.* (2nd Ed.). Chicago, IL: University of Chicago Press, 1963.

Harsh, J. R. "The Forest, Trees, Branches, and Leaves Revisited—Norm, Domain, Objective and Criterion-Referenced Assessments for Educational Assessment and Evaluation." Monograph No. 1. Fullerton, CA: Association for Measurement and Evaluation in Guidance, California Personnel and Guidance Association, February 1974.

Helmer, O. *Systematic Use of Expert Opinions.* Santa Monica, CA: The Rand Corporation, 1967.

Hencley, S. P. and Yates, J. R. *Futurism in Education.* Berkeley, CA: McCutchan Publishing Corporation, 1974.

Hewlett-Packard Company. *HP BASIC Program Library Handbook.* Cupertino, CA: Hewlett-Packard Company, 1972.

Horowitz, I. "The Academy and the Polity: Interaction Between Social Scientists and Federal Administrators," *Journal of Applied Behavioral Science,* 1969, 5, 309-335.

Institute for Social Research. *OSIRIS III.* Ann Arbor, MI: University of Michigan, 1973.

Ironson, G. H. and Subkoviak, M. J. "A Comparison of Several Methods of Assessing Item Bias," *Journal of Educational Measurement,* 16, 1979, pp. 209-225.

Isaac, S. and Michael, W. B. *Handbook in Research and Evaluation.* San Diego, CA: Robert R. Knapp, 1971.

Iversen, G. R. and Norpoth, H. *Analysis of Variance.* Beverly Hills, CA: Sage Publications, 1976.

Jacobs, G. (Ed.). *The Participant Observer.* New York, NY: G. Braziller, 1970.

Jenkins, J. J., Russell, W. A., and Suci, G. J. "An Atlas of Semantic Profiles for 360 Words," *The American Journal of Psychology,* 71, (1958), 688-699.

Jensen, A. R. *Bias in Mental Testing.* New York, NY: The Free Press, 1980.

Joint Committee on Standards for Educational Evaluation. *Standards for Evaluations of Educational Programs, Projects and Materials.* New York, NY: McGraw-Hill Book Company, 1981.

Kahn, R. L. and Cannell, C. F. *The Dynamics of Interviewing.* New York, NY: John Wiley and Sons, Inc., 1967.

Kaufman, R. and English, F. *Needs Assessment: A Focus for Curriculum Development.* Washington, D.C.: ASCD (NEA), 1975.

Kerlinger, F. N. *Foundations of Behavioral Research* (2nd Ed.). New York, NY: Holt, Rinehart and Winston, Inc., 1973.

Kirk, R. E. *Experimental Design Procedures for the Behavioral Sciences,* Belmont, CA: Brooks/Cole, 1968.

Kish, L. *Survey Sampling.* New York, NY: Wiley, 1965.

Krejcie, R. V. and Morgan, D. W. "Determining Sample Size for Research Activities," *Educational and Psychological Measurement,* 30 (April 1970), 607-610.

Leedy, P. D. *Practical Research: Planning and Design.* New York, NY: Macmillan Publishing Company, 1974.

Likert, R. "A Technique for the Measurement of Attitude Scales," *Archives of Psychology,* No. 140, 1932.

Linert, G. A. "Note on Tests Concerning the G Index of Agreement," *Educational and Psychological Measurement,* 32 (Fall 1972), 281-288.

Linstone, H. A. and Turoff, M. (Eds.). *The Delphi Method: Techniques and Application.* Boston, MA: Addison-Wesley Publishing Company, 1973.

Magnusson, D. *Test Theory.* Reading, MA: Addison-Wesley Publishing Company, 1966.

Mann, J. "Evaluating Educational Programs: A Symposium." *The Urban Review,* 1969, 3(4), 12-13.

Maxwell, A. E. "Correlational Techniques." In H. J. Eysenk, W. Arnold, and R. Meili (Eds.), *Encyclopedia of Psychology,* Vol. 1. New York, NY: Herder and Herder, 1972, pp. 221-224.

McNemar, Q. *Psychological Statistics,* (4th Ed.). New York, NY: Wiley, 1969.

Mehrens, W. and Ebel, R. (Eds.). *Principles of Educational and Psychological Measurement.* Skokie, IL: Rand McNally, 1967.

Mehrens, W. A. and Lehmann, I. J. *Standardized Tests in Education.* (2nd Ed.). New York, NY: Holt, Rinehart & Winston, 1975.

Merz, W. R. *Methods of Assessing Bias and Fairness in Tests,* ARC Technical Report No. 121-79. Sacramento, CA: Applied Research Consultants, March, 1980.

Metfessel, N. S. and Michael, W. B. "A Paradigm Involving Multiple Criterion Measures for the Evaluation of Effectiveness of School Programs," *Educational and Psychological Measurement,* 1967, 27, 931-943.

Mulaik, S. A. *The Foundations of Factor Analysis.* New York, NY: McGraw-Hill, 1972.

Nie, N. et al. *Statistical Package for the Social Sciences.* New York, NY: McGraw-Hill, 1975.

Nisbet, J. D. and Entwistle, N. J. *Educational Research Methods.* New York, NY: American Elseview Publishing, 1970.

Okey, J. R., Shrum, J. W., and Yeany, R. H. "A Flowchart for Selecting Research and Evaluation Designs," *CEDR Quarterly,* 10, (Fall 1973) 3.

Oppenheim, A. N. *Questionnaire Design and Attitude Measurement.* New York, NY: Basic Books, Inc., 1966.

Osborn, A. F. *Applied Imagination.* New York, NY: Charles Scribner's Sons, 1963.

Osgood, C. E., Suci, G. J., and Tannenbaum, P. H. *The Measurement of Meaning.* Urbana, IL: University of Illinois Press, 1957.

Patterson, J. and Czajkowski, T. "District Needs Assessment: One Avenue to Program Improvement," *Phi Delta Kappan,* December 1976, pp. 327-329.

Popham, J. W. *Criterion-Referenced Measurement.* New Jersey: Prentice-Hall, 1978.

Popham, J. W. *Educational Evaluation.* Englewood Cliffs, NJ: Prentice-Hall, 1975.

Popham, J. W. (Ed.). *Evaluation in Education: Current Applications.* Berkeley, CA: McCutchon Publishing, 1974.

Rasp, A. "Delphi: A Decision-maker's Dream," *Nation's Schools,* 92:1 (July 1973), 29-32.

Redefer, F. L. "Magnet for Ideas: Brainstorming in Education," *Saturday Review,* August 8, 1964.

Rentz, R. R. & Rentz, C. C. *Does the Rasch Model Really Work? A Discussion for Practitioners.* ERIC Report No. 67. Princeton, N.J.: ERIC Clearinghouse on Tests, Measurement and Evaluation, Educational Testing Service, 1978.

Research and Evaluation Committee ACSA. *Special Report: The Nature and Uses of Criterion-Referenced and Norm-Referenced Achievement Tests.* Burlingame, CA: Association of California School Administrators, 4, 3, n.d.

Rosenthal, R. *Experimenter Effects in Behavioral Research.* New York, NY: Appleton-Century-Crofts, 1966.

Rosenthal, R. and Jacobson, L. *Pygmalion in the Classroom.* New York, NY: Holt, 1968.

Rossi, P. "Evaluating Educational Programs: A Symposium." *The Urban Review,* 1969, 3 (4), 17-18.

Rossi, P. "Evaluating Social Action Programs," *Trans-action,* 1967, 4, 51-3.

Rossi, R. J. *Educational Researcher,* 4, 8 (September), 1975, 3-4.

Rudner, L. M., Getson, P. R., and Knight, D. L. "Biased Item Detection Techniques," *Journal of Educational Statistics,* 5 (Fall, 1980), pp. 213-233.

Russell, D., et al. *Developing a Workable Needs Assessment Process.* Los Angeles, CA: Office of Los Angeles County Superintendent of Schools, 1977.

Sackman, H. *Delphi Technique.* Lexington, MA: D. C. Heath and Company, 1975.

Sadofsky, S. "Utilization of Evaluation Results: Feedback into the Action Program," in J. Shmelzed (Ed.). *Learning in Action.* Washington: U. S. Government Printing Office, 1966.

Sax, G. "The Use of Standardized Tests in Evaluation." In J. W. Popham (Ed.), *Evaluation in Education: Current Applications.* Berkeley, CA: McCutchan, 1974.

Schnee, R. G. "Ethical Standards for Evaluators," *CEDR Quarterly,* 10, 1 (Spring 1977), 2-9.

Schulberg, H. and Baker, F. "Program Evaluation Models and the Implementation of Research Findings," *American Journal of Public Health,* 1968, 58, 1248-1255.

Scriven, M. "Evaluating Educational Programs: A Symposium." *The Urban Review,* 1969, 3 (4), 20-22.

Scriven, M. *The Methodology of Evaluation.* AERA Monograph Series on Curriculum, No. 1, Perspectives of Curriculum Evaluation, 1967.

Shaw, M. E. and Wright, J. M. *Scales for the Measurement of Attitudes.* New York, NY: McGraw-Hill, 1967.

Shoemaker, David M. "A Framework for Achievement Testing," *Review of Educational Research,* 45, 1 (Winter 1975), pp. 127-147.

Sidowski, J. B. (Ed.). *Experimental Methods and Instrumentation in Psychology.* New York, NY: McGraw-Hill, 1966.

Siegel, S. *Nonparametric Statistics for the Behavioral Sciences.* New York, NY: Mc-Graw-Hill, 1956.

Simon, A. and Boyer, E. G. (Eds.). *Mirrors for Behavior III: An Anthology of Observation Instruments.* Philadelphia, PA: Research for Better Schools, 1974.

Snider, J. G. and Osgood, C. E. (Eds.). *Semantic Differential Techniques.* Chicago, IL: Aldine, 1969.

Stenner, A. J. and Webster, W. B. *Educational Program Adult Handbook.* Arlington, VA: The Institute for the Development of Educational Auditing, 1971.

Stephenson, William. *The Study of Behavior: Q-Sort Technique and Its Methodology.* Chicago, IL: University of Chicago Press, 1953.

Stouffer, S. A. (Ed.). *Measurement and Prediction.* Princeton, NJ: Princeton University Press, 1950.

Strunk, W. and White, E. *The Elements of Style.* New York, NY: MacMillan, 1959.

Stufflebeam, D. *Needs Assessment in Evaluation.* Paper presented at the AERA Evaluation Conference, San Francisco, September 1977.

Suchman, E. A. *Evaluative Research; Principles and Practice in Public Service and Social Action Programs.* New York, NY: Russell Sage Foundation, 1967.

Test Service Bulletin No. 48. New York, NY: The Psychological Corporation, 1955.

Thomas, J. W. *Varieties of Cognitive Skills: Taxonomies and Models of the Intellect.* Philadelphia, PA: Research for Better Schools, 1972.

Thorndike, R. L. *Educational Measurement.* (2nd ed.). Washington, D.C.: American Council on Education, 1971.

Thorndike, R. L. and Hagen, E. *Measurement and Evaluation in Psychology and Education* (3rd Ed.). New York, NY: Wiley, 1969.

Thurstone, L. L. and Chave, E. J. *The Measurement of Attitudes.* Chicago, IL: University of Chicago Press, 1929.

Trow, M. "Methodological Problems in the Evaluation of Innovation." In M. C. Wittrock and D. E. Wiley (eds.), *The Evaluation of Instruction: Issues and Problems.* New York, NY: Holt, 1970, pp. 289-305.

Tuckman, B. W. *Conducting Educational Research.* New York, NY: Harcourt, Brace, Jovanovich, 1972.

Tyler, L. E. *Tests and Measurements.* (2nd ed.). Englewood Cliffs, NJ: Prentice-Hall, 1971.

Upton, G. *The Analysis of Cross-Tabulated Data.* New York, NY: John Wiley & Sons, 1978.

Van Dalen, D. B. *Understanding Educational Research: An Introduction.* New York, NY: McGraw-Hill Book Company, 1966.

Van Dalen, D. B. and Meyer, W. J. *Understanding Educational Research.* New York, NY: McGraw-Hill, 1966.

Warm, T. A. *A Primer of Item Response Theory.* U.S. Coast Guard Institute. Oklahoma City, OK, December, 1978.

Webb, E. J., Campbell, D. T., Schwartz, R. D., and Sechrest, L. *Unobtrusive Measures: Nonreactive Research in the Social Sciences.* Chicago, IL: Rand McNally, 1966.

Weiss, D. J. and Davis, R. V. "An Objective Validation of Factual Interview Data," *Journal of Applied Psychology,* 1960, 44, 381-385.

White, D. *Statistics for Education: With Data Processing.* New York, NY: Harper and Row, 1973.

Wilson, J. A., Robeck, M. C. and Michael, W. B. *Psychological Foundations of Learning and Teaching.* New York, NY: McGraw-Hill Book Company, 1974.

Winer, B. J. *Statistical Principles in Experimental Design* (2nd Ed.). New York, NY: McGraw-Hill, 1971.

Wood, R. W. "Brainstorming: A Creative Way to Learn," *Education,* November 1970.

Worthen, B. R. "Competencies for Educational Research and Evaluation." *Educational Researcher,* 1975, 4, 13-16.

Wright, B. D. & Stone, M. H. *Best Test Design.* Chicago, MESA Press, 1979.

NAME INDEX

A

Adams, R. N., 142, 150
Algina, J., 187
Anderson, J. F., 126
Anderson, N. H., 61
Anderson, R. D., 21
Anderson, S. B., 48, 61, 95, 99, 203
Antonoplos, D. P., 95
Argyris, C., 95
Arnfield, R. V., 40

B

Baker, F., 6, 9, 108
Ball, S., 48, 61, 95, 203
Berdie, D. R., 126
Berelson, B., 150
Berk, R. A., 187
Best, J. W., 113
Borg, W. R., 113, 202, 204
Boyer, E. G., 151, 152, 154
Brown, F. G., 126

C

Campbell, D., 126
Campbell, D. T., 4, 8, 9, 86, 89, 95,
    99, 135, 150
Cannell, C. F., 134
Chave, E. J., 164
Cochran, W. G., 73
Coleman, J. S., 7, 9
Collins, A., 134
Cook, L. L., 212
Coulson, D. B., 187
Cox, J., 199, 126
Cronbach, L. J., 99, 187
Czajkowski, T., 55, 56

D

Dalkey, N. C., 40
Davis, F. B., 104
Davis, R. V., 150
Dillman, D., 126
Dixon, W. J., 222
Downs, A., 6, 9
Dyer, H. S., 134

E

Ebel, R., 99, 187
Edwards, A., 195
Eignor, D. R., 212
English, A. C., 102, 104
English, F., 53, 56
English, H. B., 102, 104
Entwistle, N. J., 135

F

Fincher, C., 108
Fisher, R., 89, 204
Flanders, N. A., 153, 154
Foster, F., 212
Fox, D. J., 68, 89, 126, 134
Fox, R. S., 43
Freeman, H. E., 6, 9
Fruchter, B., 73, 195, 204, 208, 229

G

Gardner, P. L., 61
Gephart, W. J., 95
Getson, P. R., 108
Gifford, J. A., 212
Glaser, R., 187
Glass, G. V., 204, 229
Gorden, R. L., 134
Greenberg, B. G., 6, 9
Guilford, J. P., 73, 172, 195, 204,
    208, 229

H

Hagen, E., 204
Hambleton, R. K., 187, 212
Hammond, P. E., 142
Harman, H. H., 80
Harsh, J. R., 187
Helmer, O., 40
Horowitz, I., 4, 9

I

Ironson, G. H., 108
Isaac, S., 89, 101, 103, 104, 126,
    134, 176
Iversen, G. R., 208

J

Jacobs, G., 142
Jacobson, L., 95
Jenkins, J. J., 176
Jensen, 108
Jung, C., 43

K

Kahn, R. L., 134
Kaufman, R., 53, 56
Kerlinger, F. N., 89, 134, 191, 195, 208, 218
Kirk, R. E., 89
Kish, L., 73
Knight, D. L., 108
Krejcie, R. V., 73

L

Leedy, P. D., 68
Lehmann, I. J., 187
Likert, R., 168
Linert, G. A., 204
Linstone, H. A., 40

M

Magnusson, 101, 104
Mann, J., 5, 9
Maxwell, A. E., 204
McNemar, Q., 195, 204
Mehrens, W. A., 99, 187
Merz, W. R., 107, 108
Metfessel, 155, 158
Meyer, W. J., 135
Michael, W. B., 89, 101, 103, 104, 126, 134, 155, 158, 176
Morgan, D. W., 73
Mulaik, S. A., 80
Murphy, R. T., 48, 61, 95, 203

N

Nie, N., 222
Nitko, A. J., 187
Nisbet, J. D., 135
Norpoth, H., 208

O

Okey, J. R., 87, 89
Oppenheim, A. N., 126, 164, 168, 170
Osborn, A. F., 29, 31
Osgood, C. E., 173, 176

P

Patterson, J., 55, 56
Popham, J. W., 73, 181, 187
Preiss, J. J., 142, 150

R

Rasp, A., 40
Redefer, F. L., 31
Rentz, C. C., 212
Rentz, R. R., 212
Ritvo, M., 43
Robeck, M. C., 104
Rogers, W. T., 21
Rosenthal, R., 8, 9, 95
Rossi, P., 3, 4, 9, 25
Rudner, L. M., 108
Russell, D., 56
Russell, W. A., 176

S

Sachman, H., 40
Sadofsky, S., 6, 9
Sax, G., 178, 187
Schwartz, R. D., 135, 150
Sechrest, L., 126, 135, 150
Suchman, E. A., 68
Schmuck, R., 43
Schnee, R. G., 14
Schulberg, H., 6, 9
Schwartz, R. D., 126
Scriven, M., 4, 8, 9
Shaw, M. E., 164, 168, 172, 176
Shoemaker, D. M., 178, 187
Shrum, J. W., 87, 89
Shrunk, W., 234
Sidowski, J. B., 172
Siegel, S., 61, 195, 204, 218
Simon, A., 151, 152, 154
Snider, J. G., 176
Sommer, L., 8

S (Continued)

Soptick, J. M., 21
Stake, R., 7
Stanley, J. C., 8, 9, 86, 89, 95, 99, 204, 229
Stenner, A. J., 14
Stephenson, W., 49, 51
Stone, M. H., 212
Stouffer, S. A., 172
Strunk, W., 234
Stufflebeam, D., 7, 11, 54, 56
Subkoviak, M. J., 108
Suchman, E. A., 6, 89, 95
Suci, G. J., 176
Swiminathan, H., 187, 212

T

Tannenbaum, P. H., 176
Thomas, J. W., 152, 154
Thorndike, R. L., 61, 99, 204
Thurstone, L. L., 164
Trow, M., 8, 95
Tuckman, B. W., 135
Tyler, L. E., 61

U

Upton, G., 218

V

Van Dalen, D. B., 113, 135
Van Egmond, E., 43

W

Warm, T. A., 212
Webb, E. J., 126, 135, 150
Webster, W. B., 14
Weiss, C. H., 7
Weiss, D. J., 150
White, D., 222
White, E., 234
Wilson, J. A., 104
Winer, B. J., 195, 208
Wood, R. W., 31
Worthen, B. R., 21
Wright, B. D., 212
Wright, J. M. 164, 168, 172, 176

Y

Yeany, R. H., 87, 89

SUBJECT INDEX

A

AGCT scores, 228
ad hominem, 94
administration, problems of, 4
ad verecundiam, 94
analysis of variance (ANOVA):
　106, 107, 205-208
　disadvantages, 208
　F-test, 206
　purposes of, 205-206
ANOVA, *see* Analysis of Variance
alternate forms method, 98

B

behavior, classes of, 152-153
bias, definition of, 105
　procedures of detection, 106
biserial correlation, 201
blind effect, 93
BMD statistical package, 221
brainstorming:
　advantages, 31
　disadvantages, 31
　idea evaluation, 30
　procedures, 29
　rules, 29
　sessions, conducting, 30
　sessions, evaluating, 31

C

CEEB scores, 228
chi square, 106, 107
coefficient:
　biserial, 201
　correlation, 197-199
　eta, 203
　multiple correlation, 203
　Pearson, 199
　phi, 201
　point biserial, 201
　Spearman rank, 199-200
　tetrachoris, 200
coefficient correlation, 197-199
coefficient of equivalence, 102
coefficient of internal
　consistency, 103

coefficient of multiple
　correlation, 203
coefficient of stability, 102
competencies in evaluation, 23-24
confirmation research, 112
construct validity, 99
content validity, 99
context analysis, *see*
　forced field analysis
contingency table, 213-218, *see*
　cross tabulation
control variable, 66
correlation:
　coefficient, 197-199
　Pearson, 199
　Spearman ranks, 199-200
　specialized, other, 200-204
correlation coefficient, 97
correlational ratio, 203
correlational techniques, 202
cover letter, 120
criterion referenced measurements,
　177-187,
　see norm referenced measurements
criterion-related validity, 99
cross break, 213-218, *see*
　cross tabulation,
cross tabulation:
　definition, 213
　example, 218
　statistics for, 214-218
culture-bound fallacy, 106

D

data analysis, 189-222
data classification, 57-80
data gathering techniques, 115-154
Delphi technique:
　assumptions of, 37
　caveats, 38
　definition, 34
　example, 39-40
　process, 11, 34
　rationale, 33
　rounds, 35
　utilization of, 11, 37
dependent concept, 109
dependent variable, 66
descriptive statistics, 192

D (Continued)

design, methodological
    consideration, 7
directional hypothesis, 110
discrimination, definition of, 105
double blind, 93

E

elementalism, 94
egalitarian fallacy, 105
equal interval scale, 60, 161-164, *see*
    interval scale
equivalence, coefficient of, 102
equivalence, method of rational, 103
equivalent-time samples, 88
error, sampling, 146
errors, sources of, 91-94
establishment, problems of, 3
eta coefficient, 203; *see*
    correlational ratio
ethics, 13-14
expectancy effect, 93
exploratory research, 112
external validity, 144

F

F test, 193
factor analysis: 106-107
    procedures, 76-80
    steps in, 75
    types, 75
    use of, 75
fallacy:
    culture-bound, 106
    egalitarian, 105
    standardization, 106
figures prove, 93
forced field analysis, 41-43
format, reporting, 231-234
formulating hypothesis, 109-113

G

G index correlation, 201
group interview, 129
Guttman scale:
    concerns, 172
    steps, 169-172

H

HP statistical package, 221
halo effect, 93
hawthorne effect, 8, 93
hypothesis, formulating:
    development of, 111-112
    directional, 110
    null, 112
    nondirectional, 110
    relational, 110
    reporting, 110-111

I

independent concept, 109
independent variable, 65
inferential statistics, 192
internal consistency, 97, 98
internal validity, 144
interval scale of measurement, 60
intervening variable, 67
interview:
    group, 129
    preparing, 130-131
    semistructured, 129
    structured, 129
    telephone, 130
issues of evaluation, 3-13
item analysis, 101-104
item characteristic curve, 106, 107
item difficulty, 101
item discrimination, 101
item internal consistency, 102
item reliability, 102
item validity, 102

J

John Henry effect, 93

K

Kendall's *Tau,* 202

L

latent trait theory:
    advantages, 211
    assumptions, 210
    characteristics, 210
law of the instrument, 94
letter of transmittal, 120

Likert scale:
  concerns, 168
  steps, 165-168

M

matrix sampling, 72
maturation, 91
measures, multiple criterion, 155-158
measures, unobtrusive, 143-150
measurement:
  levels of, 59-61
  methodological considerations, 6
  techniques development, 18
  timing, 7
measurements, criterion-referenced,
  177-187
measurements, norm-referenced,
  177-187
measurements, reactive, 144-146
method of rational equivalence, 103
methodological considerations, 6-9
moderator variable, 66
multiple criterion measures, 155-158

N

needs assessment:
  definition, 53
  definition of need, 54
  rationale, 54
  steps in, 55
nominal scale of measurement, 59
nondirectional hypothesis, 110
nonequivalent control group, 88
nonparametric statistics, 193-194
norm referenced measurements:
  characteristics, 179-186
  definition, 178-179
  uses of, 178
  weaknesses, 181
null hypothesis, 112

O

observation techniques:
  behavior, classes, 152-153
  coding units, 153
  collection methods, 154
  components, 151
one-group pretest posttest, 84
one-shot case study, 84

ordinal scale of measurement, 60
OSIRIS statistical package, 220

P

partial correlation, 203
participant observation:
  advantages, 138
  disadvantages, 139
  rationale, 137
  steps in, 140-141
  styles of, 139-140
Pearson correlation, 199
phi correlation, 201
placebo effect, 93
point biserial correlation, 106, 107, 201
post hoc, 94
posttest-only control group, 85
pretest-posttest control group, 84
problem solving techniques, 27-56
Pygmalion effect, 93 *see*
  expectancy effect

Q

Q methodology, *see* Q-sort technique
Q-sort technique:
  basic types, 49
  procedures, 50
  statistics derived, 50
quality control, 81-113
questionnaire:
  advantages, 118
  cover letter, 120
  design, 121
  disadvantages, 118-119
  introduction, 121
  items, 122
  steps of development, 119-120
  title, 121
  validity - reliability, 119
  when appropriate, 117-118

R

Rasch model, 209-212, *see*
  latent trait theory
ratio scale of measurement, 61
rational equivalence, method of, 103
reactive concerns, 93-94
reactive measurement, 144-146

R (Continued)

relational hypothesis, 110
reliability, 97-99, 102, 119
reliability coefficient, 102-103
reliability of tests, improving the, 103
reporting format, 231-234
research, confirmation, 112
research design:
    pre-experimental, 84
    quasi-experimental, 88
    true experimental, 84-88
research, exploratory, 112
response fail analysis, 106, 107
response sets, 93
results, expressing test, 225-229
results, reporting, 223-234
results, utilization of, 5

S

sampling
    kinds of, 70-72
    matrix, 72
    selection, criteria for, 69
    size, determining, 72
sampling, error, 146
scale, Wechsler, 229
scales:
    equal interval, 161-164
    Guttman, 169-172
    Likert, 165-168
    scalogram, 169-172
    semantic differential, 173-176
    Thurstone, 161-164
scales, developing, 159-187
scalogram analysis, 169-172
scores, standard:
    AGCT scores, 228
    CEEB scores, 228
    T score, 227
    Z score, 227
secundum quid, 94
semantic differential:
    analysis, 175
    cautions, 176
    construction, 174-175
    development, 173
    uses, 174
semistructured interview, 129
Solomon four group, 85

SPSS statistical package, 220
Spearman-Brown formula, 103
Spearman ranks correlation, 199-200
split-half method, 98, 103
stability, coefficient of, 102
standard nines, 228, *see* stanines
standard scores, 227-228
standardization fallacy, 106
standards, 11-12
stanines, 228
static group, 84
statistical packages:
    BMD, 221
    characteristics, 219
    HP, 221
    OSIRIS, 220
    SPSS, 220
statistics:
    definition, 191
    descriptive, 192
    inferential, 192-193
    purpose, 191
    nonparametric, 193-194
structured interview, 129
suspended judgement, 29-31, *see*
    brainstorming

T

T scores, 227
t-test, 193
task analysis:
    bases for, 45
    precautions, 46
    steps in, 45
tasks, evaluation:
    audience identification, 17
    computer use, 19
    conclusion interpreting, 19
    data collection methods, 19
    data specifications, 16
    design selection, 16
    drawing implications, 15
    formulating hypothesis, 16
    goal identification, 17
    measurement techniques, 18
    monitoring, 18
    norm identification, 18
    objective statement, 18
    obtaining information, 15

population identification, 16
problem identification, 16
program goal assessment, 17
research reporting, 20
statistical analysis, 19
strategy selection, 16
threat recognition, 17
validity assessment, 18
variable identification, 18
techniques:
    correlational, 202
    data gathering, 115-154
    observation, 151, 154
test bias, 105-108
test-retest method, 98, 102
testing, 91
tests, expressing results, 225-229
tetrachoric correlation, 200
Thurstone scale:
    concerns, 163
    steps in, 161-163
time series, 88
transformed item difficulties, 106, 107
tu quogue, 94

U

unobtrusive measures:
    approaches, 143-144
    controlled accretion, 148
    controlled erosion, 148
    natural accretion, 148
    natural erosion, 147
unstructured interview, 128

V

validity: 97-99, 119, 144
    experimental mortality, 92
    factors jeopardizing, 91-92
    history, 91
    instrumentation, 91
    interaction effect, 92
    maturation, 91
    multiple-treatment interference, 92
    reactive effect of testing, 92
    selection bias, 92
    selection-maturation interaction, 92
    statistical regression, 91
    testing, 91
validity assessment, 18
variables:
    classification, 64
    control, 66
    dependent, 66
    kinds, 65-68
    independent, 65
    intervening, 67
    moderator, 66
    nature of, 63
    relationship of, 67
variance, analysis of, 205-208
variances, controlling, 83-84

W

Wechsler scale, 229

Z

Z scores, 227